# Trainer to Trillionaire

## From Building Memories to Building a Legacy

JASON CRIDDLE

www.voteforjason.org

www.wellnessbyjason.org

Copyright © 2014 Jason Criddle

ISBN-13:  978-0692216941 (Jason\Criddle)

ISBN-10:  0692216944

# DEDICATION

This book is for Emma. The day you started walking, you awoke a dormant superhero, and I set forth to save the world. With every step you have taken, I have kept pace, and began building you a legacy. You will never have to live the struggles I have; though I do realize you will have your own. I only hope that you can look through the turmoil and find the beauty of the world in far less time than it took me. You will forever be my baby. I love you.

Daddy

# TABLE OF AWESOMENESS

# ACKNOWLEDGMENTS

I would like to thank more people than I can possibly list. Thank you to my friends, family, and clients who have stood by me through a lifetime of trial and error. Thank you to my mentors and students. You have all taught me so much. Thank you for deciding to pick up this book and set a path towards changing your own life. If it weren't for your belief in me, I would have never accomplished all that I have today. I will never stop spreading the message we have created together. I will never stop changing the world. Thank you all. I love you very much.

# CHAPTER 1

## PROMOTING WELLNESS
## OUTSIDE OF THE GYM

### "HUSTLE UNTIL YOU NEVER HAVE TO INTRODUCE YOURSELF AGAIN. MAKE YOUR NAME KNOWN. WHY BE A MEMORY WHEN YOU CAN BECOME A LEGACY?"

I AM HERE TO WAKE YOU UP! Your mind is one of your greatest assets and I am going to open it up to a few new ideas. I love traveling the country and talking to people just as much as I love offering a different perspective once I meet those beautiful people. I have become accustomed to hearing the words, "I have never thought of it that way before." I have heard it so much, it lead me to believe I could write a book on how my entire life changed by thinking about my business in ways I, too, had never thought of before. This eventually led to the universe rewarding my efforts exponentially.

I wouldn't consider myself to be an expert at the subject matter… but I did go from being a broke pool man, to a broke personal trainer. A broke trainer to a broke speaker. Then, a broke speaker to a network-marketer. I began learning the "ins and outs" of the business and started offering my knowledge to as many people as I could. This gave people a simplified approach to seeing past the "hoopla" of the industry, and I was able to start showing people that MLM is a solid business investment. MLM is the way of the future.

Now, I travel. I talk to people and I teach them how to begin a path of financial freedom through building multiple streams of passive income, along with the wonderful people they know.

One thing I can say… these results are not typical. This book is to teach you an approach and a different perspective. There are no exact figures in here. I do plan to teach you what I have learned, but your success will ultimately depend on your course of action. If you want to learn how to dunk, and Michael Jordan decides to write a how-to book, explaining how he literally almost learned to fly, I would advise you to purchase it.

I imagine you have heard of me in some form or fashion, which is the reason you have this book in your possession. If you have been following me online, you will know I can be a bit eccentric at times. This is because I am awake! I am alive! In this world we live in, there are far too many people still asleep. Far too many people are stuck in their cyclical environment and making the same moves daily. Rarely thinking about their legacy and their future. I have found, once you are awake, it is very difficult to go back to "sheep." If you want a man to never think about his future, give him a job where his salary depends upon him never thinking about his future. Cause and effect. Ask yourself, am I causing things to happen in my life, or am I allowing things to affect me?

This is a book that you will never stop reading. A book that you will read from start to finish over and over. A book that you will read a particular chapter or sentence with highlighter, pen, and notepad right next to you, ready to catch something new. I have always found it a bit comical; we will watch a movie 30 times, which will fill our minds with negativity, then read a book that will change our life, only once. I know, because I did it for years. And you know what? As soon as I stopped doing it, I developed a vision to become a millionaire before my very next birthday.

So yes, this is a book that will forever change your approach to how you look at and market yourself. How you view your specific business as well as MLM. If you are not willing to change and adapt to our new market and our coming economy, you are going to be left behind. Give this book to your friends, and buy another copy for yourself, knowing you are only going to turn around and pass it on to another friend. And perhaps, go out and get another copy.

Never miss an opportunity to do a service for others. Never miss an opportunity to change a life. Never miss an opportunity to delve into the sheer abundance of information streaming around you. If you do not take advantage of every moment possible, to absorb as much of it as you are able, you, your business, and your ability to build your legacy will become obsolete. There is an abundance of knowledge, freely streaming through our planet... we would be ignorant to not take advantage.

An early piece of advice I will give you, is stop asking your friends and family what they think. I can almost promise you, they do not think at all. Did you know the average person thinks less than twice a year?

We are creatures of habit, trying to find the simplest way to survive. There are very few times when a conscious thought will squeeze its way into the subconscious mind for that idea to be put into action. 95% of all of that mumbo-jumbo is conditioning and programming people have been feeding you since the day you were born. Only 5% of your mind is you, working towards what you actually want.

You are the average of the five people you spend the most time with. No worse or better, just the average. So, whom are you spending time with and gathering advice from? Have these people achieved the results you want? Are these people living the life you want to live? Are they willing to take the steps necessary to change? Then why do you keep listening to them?

If you aren't getting the results you want, then POINT BLANK, something isn't working. You need to break down every single thing you are doing and find out exactly what is holding you back. You MUST take control of your life and stop allowing ignorance to hold you back. You already know what you are doing isn't achieving the results you desire... so why do you keep doing it?

Please take the time to understand, anything I ever talk or write about is coming from my very own, very limited perspective. Take a moment to do research for yourself. I don't, for a moment, believe everything that is told to me. As a matter of fact, I love being proven wrong. I love the opportunity to be wrong. I have also learned, we have a gigantic population of people who believe mostly everything they are told, without doing their own research. We mimic, and this is only causing us to continue performing conditioned behavior, and we do not even know why.

We were told to eat huge servings of grains on a daily basis. Not for health reasons, but because carbohydrates could be used as commodities and therefore, stored, traded, and sold for big bucks through the stock market. This eventually caused a couple of generations of diabetes, cancer, coronary heart disease, etc.

We are told a house is an asset, and buying a house is one of the most financially sound business decisions that can ever be made. Yes, for the bank. However, we are never told what really goes on when a house is purchased, or that a home will eventually cost us four to five times the original purchase price. We are simply mimicking the behavior of everyone else.

My perception, however, is based upon spending the majority of my life learning from as many people's perspectives as possible. Not simply befriending people and getting to know them, but learning why they made the choices they did to live their lives in a certain way. What was the "why" behind their actions? Were they paying attention to their patterns? Were they living for themselves or living in someone else's cycle? Were they willing to change in order to have what they wanted and achieve the results they desired?

By developing these habits, I learned that no one has all the answers. Especially me. So instead of living my life, feeling as though I had all of the answers, I chose to view everyone as a mentor. I became a student of life. And you can do the same. Listen and apply what you learn, or do not waste their time. Do not feel as though anyone is ever wasting your time. Only you can do such a thing. Do not give away such a great power.

The ultimate result of the change, of course, is action. Massive or drastic action. Some action will yield some results. A lot of action will yield a lot of results. It is simple mathematics. Think about every other time you gave something halfhearted effort. Did you receive the results you set out to achieve? Were your goals reached? Was the feeling of gratification fulfilled?

I took control of my life. I set a goal of saving the world and becoming the wealthiest man on the planet, and now I am well on my way. The power of belief. You write something down – you believe it is going to happen – and you begin to realize your life is a series of dots, which need to be connected. Some people believe you have to look back to see the dots. I believe, if you realize every occurrence is a dot, you can actually see your future unfolding. This will help you to connect dots more effectively, which will make you become more efficient at whatever you are striving to be. It gets really damn hard at times. You get tunnel vision. You get thrown off course. You try ideas and new strategies to grow and you sometimes fail.

Even though my business was growing, I had reached many plateaus. And plateaus do not, at all, satisfy me. While most people go through periods of days, weeks, months, or even years... my mind tends to plateau for minutes or even seconds at a time. I see a slump, find the problem, and get past the slump. No matter how good you are though, you have to dedicate your life to changing your mindset from being an employee to becoming wealthy. Our small and outright wrong beliefs in money are passed down from generation to generation, only to leave an even larger gap in upper and lower class society. We have never been taught how to work. We were never taught how to build wealth. We were never taught anything, but how to merely survive, in the world of business. We were never taught how to spend our money or pay bills. We have all been taught to be employees. We were never taught the rules of the game.

Becoming successful isn't a game. There is no amount of tickets at the carnival you can trade in to gain your self-worth. No one is going to show up at your doorstep with a box of money, ready to sign it over to you because you were playing around or because you "want" it. You can, however, take advice from someone who is doing what you want to do. If someone is willing to teach you… be willing to learn. Be willing to be wrong and start over with an empty glass.

Money isn't good. Money isn't evil. It won't buy you happiness either. It sure does make life a little easier though. Money is only a tool. Life sucked when I was broke. And I realize now that I used to say I didn't care about money because I had no money. Money is a problem, which needs to be solved. We give it value based on our needs and desires. Stop trying to acquire it, and start believing you already have it. Help more people on a daily basis, and the money will come to you. Be selfless in your actions.

Anyone, in just about any industry, can duplicate what I have done in these pages. If you focus on helping and doing good for others, wealth will come to you. Not so much in paper form, as much as the fundamental details of your life will begin to change; until your entire life has become something completely astounding. Then comes the paper.

You are the creator of your world. Nature is completely neutral and the universe is waiting for you to take action and work aggressively towards building your legacy.

People hear of the law of attraction and still have entitlements and expect handouts. The word attraction has "action" imbedded in the word. In your life, you are going to be confronted with opportunities to act, and some of those will be scary as shit! Those are usually the best ones to act upon. You need to take action, now!

Because I was a personal trainer, it made writing this book to trainers, massage and physical therapists, or gym and wellness club and nutrition store owners, a little bit easier… then I realized, anyone can apply this knowledge to their business. Do you see how helping other people, raising more capital, and adding value to one's self can help your business?

I know I am developing haters at this point in my life. And if you don't have haters, you aren't doing anything worthwhile. I spend so much time focusing on the positive change I am creating, that I never take a moment to look back at the negative. When I do run across it… I embrace it. Stay positive. Remember, you need their energy. If they are thinking about you… if they are talking about you, be it positive or negative, you are winning.

You have a computer right? Full of all of your files... precious pictures, maybe some movies. Your cherished files. Your cherished belongings. How would you react if someone came into your office, threw your computer to the ground, and proceeded to stomp it to dust? Your brain is the most powerful computer you will ever own... and you have allowed people to fill it full of shit for years.

This world as we know it. This life we think we know... it isn't real. At least our simple and misguided understanding of "real." We are an immaculate form of God's greatest creation with a brain capable of traveling into the past and future. We think unlike any other beings on the planet and we have turned ourselves into a slave race with a, "do just enough to get by" attitude. I carried this attitude for far too long and wasted many valuable years of life. Or, was it all a lesson to help lead me to where I am now? Perhaps it is the same for you?

Why am I writing this book? It needs to be written. In the 2 years I was training, I helped a little more than 500 clients lose over 9,000 pounds of fat. I lost less than a dozen out of the 500. I moved to 2 cities in 2 different states, and partnered up with some good office folks that allowed my training program to have a reach in over 100 countries. And even more countries with one particular MLM I would later be introduced to. All I had to do was get the word out.

I failed so much and made so many mistakes.

Even though my journey is still beginning, I would now consider myself to be a success... or at least on the path to. Trainer to Trillionaire is not a success story. It is an ongoing story. Compiled of literally thousands upon thousands of success stories, classes, lectures, books, and videos that helped mold my ongoing path of success.

Fun Fact: Trillionaire isn't a real word yet. Kind of tickles me. I suppose it is because the world hadn't seen the first one until I was born! Lots of work to do!

And...... back to the book.

I definitely love the "tactics" it takes to become successful, and we have plenty of time for that later. You can find "tactics and tricks," so to speak, imbedded in the pages before you. I have found, in my career, the success stories create champions, too. Building your own success story is so much a part of your own success, that I would rank it up there with action, personal development, practicing skillsets, continuing education, and most of all, belief. All of these, in addition to your journey, create your success story.

When I say belief, I, of course, mean unwavering belief. Imagine the process it would take if you were responsible for making your own body systems work. What if you controlled your own heartbeat? What if you had to mentally calculate the processes needed in order to do something as miniscule as taking a single step? You have to hardwire your dreams and aspirations of success SO DEEP inside your being, that becoming successful, and achieving whatever your level of success may be, becomes easier than walking. Success becomes hardwired. Making hundreds, thousands, or millions of dollars must be just as miniscule as taking a step.

I have developed many online mentors. Many book mentors. Many I plan to meet, some who have passed in this lifetime, and others I may never have the opportunity to meet until I pass. People of great influence who helped to mold my mind into the weapon of peace and prosperity I carry with me today. Although those names helped direct me on my path, they are not at all responsible for my success. I am responsible for my success. As you are responsible for yours.

For centuries, great inventors, speakers, business owners, life and world changers, etc., have spent countless hours, working with the unlimited potential of the expansion of the conscious mind. Once you get to this point, you realize knowledge has always been out there for the taking. It is how we apply it, that gives it value. Once you learn a new philosophy and apply it to your way of life, it then becomes yours to teach. The words are not as important as the fire they light under your ass.

Try to read books for expansion or else they will offer you the same conditioning as watching a mindless "tell-a-vision" show. If what you are reading is not expanding your mind, why are you reading it? To pass the time? Why are you passing time? How much time do you feel you have to waste? If you are going to read… take the time analyze, learn, and apply.

I questioned my existence at the age of nine. This caused me to immediately direct my focus to books. I never really cared much for the next best cartoon. Even though I loved movies, which fueled my ongoing imagination, I always drifted back towards books. I tell people, "I turned my 'tell-a-vision' off and never looked back." I spent a good part of my adolescence, reading fiction, which made me aspire to become a writer someday. I would often find an author I would like, and would read all of the books she or he had ever written. I never really cared much for picking a genre… unless an author I had grown interested in just happened to write in that particular genre.

I even do this with my movie selections. I find I tend to gravitate towards a certain director or producer and watch the films they have made rather than following a particular actor or actress.

We must remember… the author, the director, the writer, the artist; it is their story we are drawn to. They are using characters to get you to see their perspective on whatever point they are trying to get across to you. The actor is the character. And yes… a bad character can kill any story. It is the cumulative effort of all involved that make the story great. But, the story still belongs to the first person. It was one person's vision before it became the vision of many.

# CHAPTER 2

## DETACH, COLLABORATE, AND LISTEN

## "SAY SOMETHING INTELLIGENT, POSITIVE, MOTIVATING, OR INSPIRATIONAL... OR DON'T SAY ANYTHING AT ALL."

I try not to think of myself as anything special. I would say I have spent the greater part of my life reading, exploring the human mind, exploring nature, researching and educating myself on the inner workings of philosophy and theology. To this day, I remember the exact moment I questioned my existence... the exact verse and chapter I read of <u>The</u>

<u>New Testament</u>. This book isn't about religion, though, but I will say, questioning myself and my own existence sent me on a path unlike that of most people. And it still sets me apart to this day.

I began an extensive study of religion months later. By the time I had turned 13, I was well versed in quite a few different religions. I was completely fascinated by the idea of religion. Several seemed to have the same message. Come to think, in my adolescence, I often looked to pick a religious debate with someone. I never really wanted to have the "I am right and you are wrong" arguments... I merely wanted to share my knowledge with everyone.

Later in life, I would learn to have patience and compassion. I stopped debating and started listening. I learned everyone's truth is theirs to keep. I began to embrace being wrong. This was through Buddhism. Although I didn't really want to find myself identifying with a particular religion, this led me on an early path to finding myself. Clearing my mind of fear and conditioning. And beginning the practice of meditation. A clear mind and a quiet room became a craving of mine. Now, I even realize Buddhism is simply an idea.

I was an introvert my whole life. And I have a mild form of autism. Can you imagine never wanting to be around a single person for most of your life? I definitely was not shy... I opened up. However, opening up was the last activity on my list of things to do.

One of the coolest gifts I taught myself during this time; gifts, skills, whichever you choose to call it... was detachment. I learned this by letting go of fear of judgment at such a young age. I grew up without a full-time dad. I felt I was the outcast of my family. I never attended church or family bible studies. If it took place outside of my bedroom, I wanted nothing to do with it. I began living the life of a hermit. An introvert. The age of detachment began.

I developed a habit of observing rooms since I spent so much time in mine. While someone would normally see an average room with organized clutter and obvious footprints of someone's life – I would analyze the room as a detective and start making a mental checklist of attributes about the person. As a pool man, my last few years in the industry were spent working on foreclosed homes. It is sad to say, but I could often be in someone's home for less than a minute before figuring out exactly why they were evicted. There were times when it was really sad. Heart wrenching at times. Others... you could just tell.

All of this ultimately led up to being able to analyze behavior. By detaching from myself, I developed a habit of imagining my own life being followed by a camera... and I began looking at my life from the position of an interviewer. If I were walking, driving, eating, talking, etc., I imagined a camera above me and a stenographer (of sorts) on the other side of the camera. Following me and recording my every movement. To be broadcasted to my audience worldwide.

I developed the habit of asking myself "what should I be doing?" I began talking to people the same way and treating others equally. Whether it were friends, family, or now, my clients; I could offer advice, listen, and give unbiased opinions. I developed a neutral mind and became emotionally resilient.

In this industry, people come to us because they trust us. It is easy for someone to take the position of greed and start using that relationship for a darker gain. Always make sure you detach. Take a look at all problems your client is laying out before you. Nutrition, exercise, finances... relationships. Some of them do not even need an answer, they just need you to lend an ear. That said, do not open your mouth unless your audience would approve of what you are about to say. Do not, ever in life, hurt someone to satisfy your ego. Call it, advanced ambition.

I love that we can take a moment to look back on our lives and connect the dots. Questioning my life led to my finding motivational speakers to act as mentors, instead of a deity. I strived to achieve more for myself. To constantly search for new ladders of vitality to climb. I sought out new goals to reach that others may have considered to be unreachable. Hardships were just as welcomed in my life then as they are today. All of those decisions eventually led up to this book. Imagine that.

# CHAPTER 3

## BE EFFECTIVE OR BE FORGOTTEN.

## "IF YOU ARE AFRAID OF SOMEONE STEALING YOUR BUSINESS, YOU DON'T KNOW HOW TO RUN YOUR BUSINESS."

My entire life, I thought of myself as a businessman. I have had hundreds of jobs and hobbies. Constantly developing an extreme interest in something and focusing all of my time and effort on my new interest, until I mastered it, and then I would move on. I realized later in life, I was not only accumulating knowledge to get me to this point, I was also living my path. Finding my path. So many of us are afraid of change, but you have to take a broad look at your life.

Are you getting the results you are looking for? Are you willing to change in order to achieve the level of success, or results, you are looking for? Are you willing to change as many times as it takes in order to achieve the results you so desire?

I changed my field; I changed my craft, because I was looking for a certain result. That result, was freedom.

A good friend of mine asked me, "What satisfies you?"

This was a good friend of mine who was a mentor in my eyes, even though he was only 19 years old to my 30. (We are so quick to judge the opinions of others. Thinking they are wrong and we are right. If we take the opportunity to be wrong and learn from every word spoken to us, we can become a completely unique individual. We can become the mentor.)

He went on about how he had asked a few people about their level of satisfaction, and the answers he received were not on the same level as his own. Not in a positive or negative way, just a different perspective. As he was always one to embrace the differences as well as similarities in people, I loved hearing his viewpoints.

He said, most of us are satisfied by a car, a boat, a

career, a new cell phone, a home. Maybe even a new relationship, or marriage. This did not satisfy him. What satisfied him was knowledge. He said, if you take everything away, all you have left is the knowledge you have acquired and what you do with it. If you are left alone, you only have the thoughts you are able to manifest... and the ideas you place upon those thoughts.

Education vs. Validation. I spent many years of my life trying to look for validation and approval from others. I realized I was going out there and trying to get people to think "my way" was right, rather than merely sharing my perspective. But only because I was insecure with myself. I was constantly changing my way of thinking, reacting to situations, turning into a completely different person when looking for companionship, and never being my true self. I spent all of my life being the person other people wanted me to be, which is why I spent most of my life unhappy, and reading alone in an empty room. On the flip side, I was also NOT applying the knowledge I was acquiring because I was still too busy listening to other people and trying to conform for their benefit.

You have to be your own hero. Become whoever it is you want to be. I was meeting with a good friend of mine who spent 20 years in the food industry and left to take his first shot at selling insurance. He was worried about the amount of time and policies it would take in order for him to reach the income potential he wished to reach.

He mentioned he could get there faster if he were in front of people inside higher income brackets but he needed to start small so he could continue getting better at his craft and then attack the big fish later.

You don't get better at attacking the big fish later if you do not go after the big fish now. This is simply a lack of confidence. A lack of belief in one's self. This is the same as someone offering discounts, or, devaluing their very own service. You know exactly what you are capable of. Become it. Every single day. When you are feeling stressed out... stop. Breathe. Think. No matter how bad the day may seem, you will get through it. You've done it thus far.

Enjoy my story, follow my story, and then, create your own story. Everyone in every industry can adapt this perspective... you can take any of these ideas and run with them. We all have something to sell. Create your ending and take steps every single day, working diligently towards that ending or goal. If you know where you are heading, at least you have a direction. Learn from everyone and everything.

Any personal trainer in the world can duplicate what I have done. Any entrepreneur can adapt the same philosophies. Anyone can create their own level of success. Their level of satisfaction. Be it, a millionaire, billionaire, or even a new homeowner. No dream is too big or too small.

We all get into business for different reasons. We seek the path of employment or self-employment... business owner or investor. Regardless of what we are doing, we are doing it because we need to make money. Unfortunately, most people have the wrong ideas of how to attract money to them and/or make money work for them. I can assure you, if you are trying to work hard for your money rather than work smart for your money, you will never get ahead. Ever.

You must learn how to learn before you can expect to learn how to teach, so it is time to clear your mind.

I used to weigh close to 300 pounds. I started doing "they said" science. Going into the gym and doing 3 sets of 12 because "they" said to do it. Or changing my diet based on things "they" told me to do. After a while, I realized "they" were idiots. "They" are nobody and we make "them" up in our heads based upon ideas we have heard or read somewhere. We then try to validate these ideas by doing the 3rd party blame tactic. (I am not the expert, but if I can lead you to believe someone else is, maybe it will validate me.) No one really knows who "they" are. The more I spoke, the more I gave away my lack of education.

So, I am 300 pounds, and I starve myself and do cardio, all the way down to about 185 pounds. I had loose skin everywhere. No muscle mass. Still had tons of body fat in places I did not think body fat was supposed to be any longer. I was tired; I was unhealthy because I did it the wrong way. So I quit starving myself. I quit running miles and miles every day, and within 6 months, I jumped all the way up to

390 pounds. I never will know my exact weight, because it fluctuated based on the 10 pounds of food I could have eaten or not eaten that day.

Eye opening.

I then went into a gigantic box gym and I was sold on training. What do I mean I was sold? I was told a fancy story. I signed on the dotted line. Money was pulled from my account for months and months and I never showed up to the gym. Not a single time. I wasn't ready. And that's ok. A lot of people aren't ready when they first start.

Fortunately for me, when I was ready to make the change, I had saved up over 100, paid-for, personal training sessions with the gym.

I had different times in my life where my weight varied. But in 2011, when my daughter started walking, I decided to walk back into that big corporate gym and work with a personal trainer. I won't, right now, go into detail about every single thing that influenced my decisions... but my life needed a change. I HATED my job and had a daughter to raise. It was time to change.

Originally, I had gone through about half a dozen trainers. Clipboard holders and rep counters. Trainers who cared more about their cell phones and friends in the gym than the progress of their clientele. It took a little while, but I finally found a trainer who befriended me and helped me to not only believe in myself, but find the passion behind going to the gym and working out. It was passion and drive that helped me become better and start my weight-loss journey, so I committed to finding this in my clients.

I can give 10 clients a diet and workout regimen. The 9 who look at it as a chore will fail. The 1 that wants to be better, regardless of pain or consequence, will win. About a year and 100 pounds into my weight-loss, I realized I wanted to be a personal trainer. It was completely unlike any career path I had taken up to that point in my life, but I wanted to take the leap and dive right into the education required to get started.

At this point, I had made a temporary trip across the country to Georgia to live with my brother for a few months. There was a small neighborhood gym that I began working out in within days of my arrival. With my mindset and my knowledge, I really considered myself to be a big fish in a small pond. When I decided to move back to Dallas, I thought I was going to be a small fish in a big pond, so to speak.

Going back into the gigantic box gym where I had lost all of my weight, I realized it only had to do with me. Who you are as a person is all that matters. Not the place, or even the size of the place. Being a great trainer didn't have anything to do with continuing education or certificates or anything in that realm. You just had to be good with people in order to be successful in this business. This will more than likely hold true with any business for that matter.

**CHAPTER 4**

**A FEW KEYS TO SUCCESS**

**"WINNERS ARE PEOPLE WHO ACHIEVE THEIR GOALS MORE OFTEN"**

Happiness is not a long-term goal. It is a choice... no different than any other choice you can make. And that very choice is going to be a major key in building relationships with other people as well as yourself. It is so refreshing to meet a total stranger who is taking the time out of their day to be overly friendly to fellow strangers. While some may think this is a cry for attention, I feel this person is truly free and aware of their own free will, true self, and purpose. If you have to convince yourself that you are happy... keep working. Your happiness needs to be as strong as your belief. Unwavering, no matter how unstable the foundation around you may seem to be. Love is the gateway and truth to happiness. He who does not hear the music, thinks the dancer crazy. Your journey to success will be in front of you for the rest of your days. How will you treat those around you?

Success too, will never have a stopping point. After redirecting my focus, and changing the people I associated with throughout the many courses my life took, I began analyzing some of the major behavioral characteristics of some of the wealthiest and most successful people I surrounded myself with. Not as to compare them to others... just to see what set them apart. All those with whom I engaged, were interested and interesting, curious, inclusive, attentive, open, and humble. It struck me that those are not generally qualities or characteristics we apply to masters of the universe. Quite the contrary, we more often use words such as self-centered or egocentric. Maybe even boring, dull, or bland. Even when I was nearly 400 pounds, I used to think of fit or in-shape people to the same degree. After becoming fit myself, I realized reality was quite different – the exact opposite in most cases.

We should always look for opportunities to reconsider our perception about others... especially when questioning or analyzing effective roles of leadership and how these leaders may conduct themselves inside and outside of their businesses. Sometimes we must seek out a person's best traits in order to find and learn from them.

What makes a person successful? I do not believe there is a definitive master list. If there were a list, it would always be added to, by numerous people from all over the globe. One trait that sets a winner apart from the rest, is they look for and find opportunities where others see nothing. We, as humans, find what we are looking for. If we are craving an immediate desire for success, our environment will shift in order to deliver us that success. You must still work hard though, for this shift to take place.

You must find a lesson where others will only see a problem. You realize by now, anything and everything that happens to us, can be an opportunity to learn from. Stay focused on creating solutions and results, rather than solving problems. This way, you will only encounter solutions and results. Problems will become welcomed circumstances. Deal with your problems and challenges quickly and effectively. Don't put your head in the sand. Face your challenges and use them as opportunities to grow and learn more about yourself. You can tell the size of the man by the size of the problem he allows to bother him.

Obscurity is definitely killing you. As of right now, you are nobody, to everybody. You must spend time not only bettering yourself, but making yourself known to other people. You must spend a considerable amount of time establishing your own credibility. Work on active marketing rather than passive marketing. Passive marketing is putting out ads, blogs, signs etc., and hoping someone will take notice and get back with you. Active marketing is getting out there and getting in front of people. Shaking hands. Talking in person.

Emails, texts, and even the phone, are all tools that will limit your success if you allow them to. Never underestimate the power of talking to someone in person. This will invoke true feeling and emotion. You will leave yourself less of a chance for any miscommunication.

Keep a mental log of what works and what doesn't, that way, you waste zero time on what no longer serves you. For example, if you have a flawless sales script, and it takes you three minutes to get to the point to where you keep losing stability, and then lose the prospect – become completely efficient at the first 3 minutes. Practice it so much that it becomes muscle memory – an afterthought. Now you can focus your effort on driving past that mistake. If you keep staring at a tree, you will veer towards the tree. Get rid of the tree completely. Visualize the path, and stay productive on the path.

You must surround yourself with like-minded people. Discover the importance of synergy and start creating win-win relationships. There are many benefits from being part of a bigger team. No matter how many ideas one person can come up with, more people can come up with more ideas. More perspectives can find more innovative solutions to existing ideas. You are the average of the five people you spend the most time with. Be sure to surround yourself with people who see your vision, and have your ultimate goals in mind as well. Even if they are not walking the path with you, they should at least be a part of your award-winning support team.

DO NOT SURROUND YOURSELF WITH TOXIC PEOPLE. Average people are attracted to and comfortable with other average people. Do you wish to remain average?

Remember, you and only you create your success. You must become consciously and methodically aware of your vision, and work your ass off to create it. Others seem to hope success will find them. You seek, so you shall find.

You must overcome fear. We are taught throughout our lives to be fearless. Fear is not only necessary, it makes us stronger. Fight or flight mode is created by the feelings and emotions we place upon a given situation. And that situation is usually one which will allow us to grow into a greater person. This is why we feel the initial bout of fear to begin with. This is your body, being faced with what used to be a limitation, and your mind, being given the ability to decide to finally overcome it. All too often, we look for ways to go around. Then we never become better. A successful person is just as fearful as everyone else, however, they are not controlled or limited by their fears. They look for opportunities to break these barriers down.

You must ask the right questions. You must limit yourself from certain thoughts and situations to allow room for the right thoughts and situations. Only ask questions which will place you in a productive, creative, and positive state of emotion.

Do not complain. Do not place blame on others. This will only place you in a negative state of mind. Not only is it a waste of emotions, it is a waste of energy. (inner-chi) A negative state of mind is an unproductive state to be in. The time you are spending not taking responsibility for your actions and outcomes, or lack thereof, is time you could be creating, planning, and/or serving other people.

Make up what you lack in talent with skill. And practice that skill, with a ridiculous work ethic. Most successful people find proficient ways to maximize their potential. The key to simplification is duplication. Achieving the maximum amount of results with as little effort as possible. This will take practice. Be willing to outwork and outsmart everyone. Use every available resource you have more effectively.

There is a huge difference between being productive or proactive, and being busy. A job keeps you busy. If you want to keep a man from thinking about his future, give him a job where his salary depends on him never thinking about his future. Even sitting around thinking, reading, or watching television can be proactive if you are actually learning from, then applying what you have learned.

Becoming successful takes living. Not merely surviving. You must have ambition to ride the ride of sheer amazement. Why live your life on autopilot when you can take control? You must create clarity and certainty about what you want (and don't want) in your life. Take time to visualize and plan out your reality. Create the ending to your story and take active steps to direct your life. Most people are spectators of theirs. Do you want to be a spectator of yours?

Always innovate. Never imitate. If you are going to take the time to make something better, follow through. Giving something half of the effort will give you half of the results. You are unique to this world. To this universe. To creation as we know it. You and only you have your gift, and you and only you can share your gift with the world.

**"Either write something worth doing, or do something worth writing." – Benjamin Franklin**

Successful people refuse to procrastinate and don't spend their life waiting for the "right time." I find far too many people waiting for their big break. What is a big break? I have heard far too many times, the answer to someone's financial woes are either winning the lottery, or they are waiting for "something big" to happen to them. The problem with this is, no one ever has any valid points to support their argument of what "something big," really is. If you are waiting for the perfect time, or the right time to make something happen, you will more than likely take your ideas to your grave. I believe in fate, destiny, chance, luck... however, I will not wait for any of these ideals to determine or shape my future. I believe in, and I am committed to actively and consciously creating my very own best life and best self.

Become a life-long learner – become the master student. You must constantly work at educating yourself, either formally, (academically) informally, (watching, listening, asking, reading, being a student of life) or experientially... (doing, trying) or a combination of the three.

Remain the optimist, even (especially) if you stand alone. While some may call this, the glass half full mentality, I prefer to think, at least there is something in the glass. Truth be told, if I were hard at work and two people were sitting around arguing about the glass being half full or empty, I would drink the water and get back to work.

If you only grind on the days you feel like grinding, you won't get much done. Consistently do what you need to do, irrespective of how you may feel on a given day. If you are tired of starting over, stop quitting. Successful people rarely live a life of stopping and starting. They live a life of going.

Take risks. Calculated risks... not unnecessary risks. Financial, emotional, professional, psychological. Step outside of the box. Do things others would never be willing to do. Don't get yourself hurt and do not hurt others in the process.

Many people are reactive. Stay proactive. Think like a chess player. Always stay a few moves ahead. Think about the amount of things that will cease to "happen" to you if you are only focused on making things happen for you. Think about the amount of energy you can direct towards your future goals rather than fixing past mistakes. Take action before taking action is necessary.

Do not be a slave to your emotions. Just like fears, successful people feel emotions too. However, they are no longer slaves to their emotions. They stay in a state of being which will only serve the good of themselves and others.

Be an effective communicator. Take active steps to become a more effective speaker. There are classes, networking groups, books, seminars, dvds… virtually endless amounts of correspondence available for you to learn from so you can get your message across to your audience. Regardless of what message you wish to get across, you must be understood. You must amaze them. You must be able to give them reason to listen to you, believe in you, and want to be a part of your vision.

The act of planning is necessary. I do not believe a well thought out plan is something that is put on paper to reference every step of the way. I believe a well thought out plan requires a brief moment of brainstorming followed by drastic action. You will need to have a plan for your life and work methodically at turning that plan into a reality. Your life should no longer be a series of unplanned events and outcomes.

I mentioned this earlier, but your desire to be exceptional means that you are typically going to do things that most others will not do. You become exceptional by choice. Successful people, who are too busy doing, will rarely make time to talk to you about what you are not doing. Success will lie forever dormant, until you "do." Doing will lie forever dormant, while you are talking about it. There are no coincidences. Only opportunities that can set your life on a completely different course, and thoughts and fears that can kill those opportunities. We're all faced with life-shaping decisions on a daily basis. Successful people make the decisions that most won't and don't make.

Many people are pleasure junkies and not only lack self-control, they also avoid pain and discomfort at all costs. Successful people understand the value and benefits of working through the tough times that most people actively avoid. Any opportunity to learn is a good opportunity. An opportunity to change your mind is a better one. Always take advantage of those moments when you can practice self-control. Understand the importance of discipline in your actions and be happy to take the road less travelled.

Identify your core morals and values and do your best to live a life in accordance to those values. Do not push these values on other people as much as you will simply make them aware of your values, and let it be known that you will not deviate from these core beliefs without proper knowledge and consideration.

Introduce yourself to the idea of balance. Those who are only successful on a financial level, are not happy at all. People who are only happy in a relationship, are not successful at all. There is no balance. Money and success are not interchangeable. We live in a society that teaches us that money equals success. Like many other things, money is a tool. It's certainly not a bad thing, but ultimately, it's just another resource to gain access to what it is you really want. Too many people worship money while their focus should be on having a reason or meaning behind needing money. Balance in wealth comes when you have created an environment of stability and happiness. Everything you touch turns to gold because of what you can do for others, not yourself.

Be humble, secure in your skin, and never forget your roots. Be confident in your abilities, but not arrogant. Your sense of worth is not derived from what you own, whom you know, where you live, or what you look like. Your sense of worth comes from how you make others feel when in their presence. Never, for a moment, believe you are better than anyone or anything else. Remain generous and kind. Always take pleasure in uplifting others and making them look good, as well as helping others achieve their goals and dreams. Be happy to admit to mistakes and apologize when needed. Remember, we are mere reflections of the people who are right in front of us.

Be adaptable and embrace change. Nature forces us to find a balance of comfort and habit. Become comfortable with the new and the unfamiliar.

To be successful you will also want to keep yourself in shape physically. I know that I used to be a trainer and a competitive athlete, so this is not to be mistaken with training for the Olympics or being obsessed with your body – unless it serves you. You want to have a basic understanding of the importance of being physically well. Your body is not who you are, but it is where you live. It is YOUR temple.

You will want to have a bigger and stronger engine than everyone. Laziness should not be a word in your vocabulary. Outlast everyone. Become completely resilient to the idea of failure. Most people rarely warm up. Few would prefer to throw in the towel. You are just warming up. But also practice using your off switch. Know when to relax... remember what you have, what you are doing, why you are doing it, and have a blast doing it too. Do not waste time getting read, rather, remain ready.

Embrace haters. Embrace feedback. Embrace constructive criticism. Embrace negative criticism. The people who do not like us will offer a different perspective than those who love and follow us. Listen to and act upon feedback. These tests are here for you to become better. Stop investing time and emotional energy in things you have no control over. Instead, become aware and act accordingly. A hater, will never be as successful, as you. Successful people do not hate. Period.

Become comfortable spending time alone. Do not respond to everything and everyone. Your time is important. Spend a good amount of your day in solitude, thinking, or even practicing mediation. Most men's problems stem from his inability to sit alone in a quiet room. We are all multi-dimensional, amazing, wonderfully complex creatures. Not only physical and psychological beings, but emotional and spiritual creatures as well. Consciously work at being healthy and productive on all levels, even when lost in thought.

Set higher standards for yourself and if others do not meet those standards, distance yourself from them. Higher standards produce a greater commitment, more momentum, a better work ethic and, of course, better results.

Look for more ways to succeed. Don't rationalize failure. While many are blaming their limitations; their age, their sore back, their lack of time or opportunities, their poor genetics, or their "bad luck," you will be finding ways to succeed despite any challenges.

Lastly, successful people practice what they preach. Their career is not their identity; it's their job. It's not who they are, it's what they do. They are more interested in taking on tasks effectively, more so than taking the easy way out. They don't just talk about theory, they live in it. They live in reality; in constant search of the next course of action that will produce the best result over the long term. Implementing this will allow you to finish what you start. While so many spend their life starting things that they never finish, successful people get the job done. Even if/when the novelty and excitement has worn off.

# CHAPTER 5

## UNDERSTANDING VALUE

## "IF YOU ARE WORKING FOR THE WEEKEND, YOU ARE WASTING 71% OF YOUR LIFE."

Value is exactly this – how you value, perceive, carry, portray, and, overall, believe in yourself. Many people are confused with the idea that being a personal trainer gives them value, or being a chiropractor or a doctor, a nurse or a teacher, gives them value. It is actually the other way around. There are many people walking the planet with the positions or titles you choose to give yourself. However, make no mistake – you are the one adding value to the title.

Your job title is the last thing that matters when it comes to you. It is not who you are or what you are made of. Who you are and what you are made of is what adds value to your job. Sure, they can sign up with any trainer, but this is why they will see results with you. Sure, they can go to any chiropractor, but this is why they will become pain-free with you... the list goes on and on.

Do not offer discounts. Do not devalue yourself. Offering something for free is service. If you are offering service to not only fulfill the laws of the universe, but also bring more attention and value to your business, that is one thing. To give someone a price for the position you have allowed yourself to get paid for, and then offer discounts, or devalue yourself, can show a lack of confidence in your ability to lead or direct. Some will say... well, I will only discount in the beginning...

No you won't. You will find yourself in the trap of forever offering discounts to friends, family, associates, etc. Set a price and stick with it. You are worth it.

You need to take a moment to remember why you got into business anyway. Think about this... all of your life's decisions led to filling out that job application. Or even to filling out the loan application to your bank when you decided to take the plunge into being self-employed. Do you remember why you took the plunge? Do you remember what button was being pushed that started this cycle of behavior? Are you spending all of your days thinking about the cycle of wake up – work – sleep – repeat?

No, YOU are not. You have value. Unlike everyone else in your field, what sets you apart is what you can offer. No one... and I mean, no one, can do it like you. Speak, create, lend, teach, and do! It does not matter what line of work you have chosen for yourself, all of the value you need to add to any task is within you. Keep listening to your mentors. Keep saying your affirmations. Keep doing personal development until you wake up and realize you are the teacher. You are the mentor and the guru. You have the ability to create anything you wish to create, so go create it. Empower your beliefs with action.

In order to be a successful entrepreneur, you have to out work and out think everyone in your field. Business is 24/7 and the world your competition. Never make it about money... or even think for a second it is all about the money. To me, it is about teaching people things they don't know, and learning about topics they aren't willing to learn. When I have the opportunity to speak about it, it makes me stronger as a speaker, a thinker, and a believer. I add value to my speeches, or to my role of educating people on changing their lives, by self-education and waking up every single day with a promise to myself to be better than I was yesterday. A promise to make real change in the world. To be a better mentor, a better father, a better man, and a better human. As long as I work on myself and not the task at hand, the line of people in front of me, whom are waiting for my help, grows.

All of the value you will ever need is you. Spend as much time as possible adding as much value to as many lives as you possibly can. That means, be awesome and help other people!!

When I got started at my gym, there were about 22 trainers, from my count, in and out of the gym. Full and part-time. Within 2 weeks of being there, this number had been taken down to 9. What was the reason for this? Simple. I had stepped up the level of game in the gym. Meaning the clients in the gym were actually getting results. A ripple was caused because of the belief I had in my own abilities.

A lot of trainers probably realize by now, that some trainers suck! And while there are a TON of excellent trainers out there, there are just as many misunderstood apples. People will literally choose a trainer over price. Not just price, but haggle over miniscule amounts of money. Others will pick someone based on sexual attraction or how a trainer looks. While aesthetics play a role in this industry too, a proven track record takes precedence over any reason you can come up with. Anyone interested in personal training should be interested in an effective program with proven results. This is a huge decision. A huge step in a whole slew of tiny steps you must take to change that life of yours... do you care about anything else except your results? Anyone can give you a price. Not everyone can give you results. Anything else is a bonus acquired with the original decision.

Regardless of what kind of trainer you see yourself as; corporate gym trainer, a bodybuilder, physique competitor, swimsuit model, general health and wellness coach; you need to be effective. You need to get your clients results. Your focus, should be their results. You should eat, sleep, and breathe their results. You want to become a master at creating a system that can create results. If someone wants to become a bodybuilder, they should see someone who has produced, duplicated, and recreated bodybuilders over and over again. That isn't to say a trainer with a specialization in underwater basket weaving will not be effective, but for the most part, the trainer with a proven system will get you results. Since I had lost 200 pounds myself through my career, I am certain you can guess what I was best at. I had all different types of clientele. I had swimsuit models, collegiate athletes, people who wanted to pack on muscle. I did metabolic resistance and even bodybuilding, but I was best at shaving pounds off of those who had spent most of their life on giving up on themselves.

I become a pro at perceived rate of exertion, motivating and pushing, keeping track of results and workouts, simply because I had lived it before. And I actually took the time to know and care about my client. How many trainers actually hear the words their clients are saying? Carrying on long-winded conversations with their client and interrupting their workout to engage others? Now, how many trainers listen? Listen without expecting to respond?

Listen without thinking you are the message, rather, only a messenger. Sometimes you need to pay more attention to what is going on with your client's life rather than being focused on the books and the procedures at the gym. If there are conversations taking place, they need to be bettering your client's life. Remember... results. If you are holding up someone's progress, you are going to be the first person to take the blame. As you should.

A year and a half into my career, I directed my attention to "volunteer for knowledge," at a couple of gyms doing metabolic resistance programs. I became highly involved and also fell in love with the trainers as well as each and every member of these gyms. And I am still thankful to this day, for that opportunity.

With one in particular, I watched growth from infancy. When I started, there were 10 clients, and then I saw 25, then 50, and saw it fall back to 10. The problem was, basic periodization of the human body. The clients would get into the program, lose a bit of water weight, then plateau for months on end. They were never taught how to pull out of this plateau. Or to mix the program with other forms of conditioning as the coaches themselves did daily. And unfortunately, as it was not my program, my input was limited for quite some time.

The program I was involved in had a few major flaws. This should have been a sport. Not a strength and conditioning program for average gym-goers. The average person "could" get in shape from following the program, though it was not nearly as effective as other proven programs, like bodybuilding, HIIT, or even martial arts conditioning. This was completely apparent throughout the industry. The programing was great, but it was originally designed to take an existing athlete and condition their body to the point of having utilizable strength, rather than useless muscle mass. But, that was not the major flaw.

The program was even known for its amount of injuries. If you use any search engine and look up the program, you would find more negative than positive any day of the week. But, I realized, it wasn't the sport, it was the individual coaches and the limiting ideas they were putting into the programming. If you are teaching your students with a limited perspective and unwilling to adapt to different philosophies, your students will suffer and their target results will not be achieved. That still wasn't necessarily the biggest flaw, either.

The flaw, and reason for failure... the clients, who were not getting results, were not being listened to. Their voices and concerns were never heard because they were being overshadowed by the belief that one way, was the correct way. The only way. Concerns were not being addressed because they went against the status quo of the program. And instead of the coaches looking for innovative and proactive solutions, they were busy reacting and losing clients.

Nothing was being individualized for any one particular client. Instead, the clients were being lead to believe the systems in place could achieve results for anyone, so if they were not seeing results, it was their fault... not that of the program.

The program eventually went back to bare bones. I spent a short time in the other metabolic program, and eventually went back out on my own.

# CHAPTER 6

## WHICH CERTIFICATION(S) WILL BEST SERVE ME?

## "YOU SHOULD NEVER BE AFRAID OF A CAREER CHANGE. YOU SHOULD BE MORE AFRAID OF BECOMING SUCCESSFUL AT A CAREER THAT DOES NOT MATTER."

There are literally dozens of schools that provide education to trainers and those interested in becoming trainers. You can look online, ask someone at the gym, or even throw a rock in some instances and hit a school willing to teach someone how to become a personal trainer. You can even take courses in high school and college now. There are two different people who care about these certifications more than anyone else (from my perspective); big box gyms, for insurance purposes – and new trainers, usually for some sort of ego trip or bragging rights.

You need to start somewhere. There is nothing wrong with being the beginner or being viewed as the beginner. There are a lot of people who will give the beginner or underdog a shot, if they see the underdog's passion. Trying to become the immediate expert may work in some industries, but when it comes to changing the human body, you have to pay your dues. You need trial and error. You need to fail until you learn what works best for you and your clients.

I had already taken the trip down self-education lane before ever making a decision to pick an actual accredited school for my certification, not to mention, I was already working out with my own trainer. This worked well in my favor because I had already spent months in forums, blogs, chat rooms, etc., always in search of the next best school. Gathering knowledge beforehand not only helped me to pick my school based on my own analysis, but I picked one based on my actual goals rather than taking the suggestions of someone with an agenda that differed from mine.

All of the schools have their benefits. Reading 5 different books will give you 5 different perspectives. Rather than thinking one may be better than the other, you can embrace the differences in them all in order to become a more effective trainer. Get the certification that is necessary to get you started on your journey. Learn the systems, learn the workouts, and learn the form and physiology of it all. Embrace it all. Then go out there and apply the knowledge. Don't fall into what I call, "paralysis by analysis." You can spend all of the time in the world focused on the education… that doesn't necessarily mean you will be an effective trainer. Especially if you haven't yet worked with any clients. Remember that.

Believe it or not, you can actually spend way too much time reading and not enough time going out there and seeing what you've got. Apply your knowledge while you are getting to know people, so you can get better at your craft while you are already surrounding yourself with new people.

One instance, I had a new trainer working with me. He had never worked in any field except retail, and he only had his certification for a couple of weeks. After working with me for a week, he approached me after class. He had taken note of the type of person I was. How I engaged my clients as well as other trainer's clients and how they engaged me in return. He had witnessed the overall camaraderie of the team we had created and saw the results with his own eyes. He asked me, "What certifications do I need to focus on, in order to become the trainer you have become?"

After a few minutes of consideration, the only answer I could give him was, psychology. Nothing that made me the person I was, came from a training book. It came from the overall person I had decided to be in my life at that point. He did not need to focus on becoming a trainer like me. He needed to focus on becoming a trainer like him.

There is no NEXT LEVEL. There is no ultimate. There is only you. There are specializations, of course, but even the specialists need to "know" people, in and out in order to be successful. Take the time to learn human behavior. Take the time to practice listening to your client. I can guarantee no matter what ailment you can get a specialized certification to work on… at the other end of that certification, is the human being with which you will be working.

In a way, the certification is your gateway to getting into the corporate environment and conforming to a systematic style of running a gym. You will gain access to all of the balance balls and purple dumbbells you can get your hands on. If you take a moment to think about all of the box gyms out there, even though some have their niche, they all pretty much follow the same guidelines. They all have the same prices and training programs. There are no tailor-made regimens for the clients, unless they are fortunate enough to have a trainer with the passion to create a regimen for them. You just have to ask yourself, is this serving you?

There is nothing wrong with the system per say, however, it is a system built to create income for the gym. It is built for the corporation's success. Not for yours. Do you feel it is in your best interest to become successful at this system? You should never be afraid of a career change. You should be more afraid of becoming successful at a career that does not matter.

These gyms usually have the same trainers. There are a few in there who are going to make it big. And the trainers who are going to make it big, are going as fast as they came because they realized it was a stepping stone to exactly what they did NOT want their personal training program to represent. Time and time again, I have talked to, and even interviewed on camera, many a trainer, overly frustrated with the same process.

Please do not take this as me saying you should not pursue further education avenues in your training career. What it boils down to; most of the schools are going to do the same thing for you. It is ultimately up to you to get results for your clients. When you are in a one-on-one with your client, your focus should be one thing and one thing only... getting results for said client. In a big gym or on your own, without results, you will not be a trainer for long.

Naturally, results equal happy clients. Happy clients mean more revenue for the gym. In the gym at which I was training, results equaled more gym revenue. So, eventually, they wanted to take me from the position of trainer and move me to the management side. Even though I was a trainer, I was now making more revenue for the gym than the commission-based sales personnel. Sometimes selling two to three times the amount of product, week after week, to the clients they were supposed to be selling to. Once being moved to the management side, I knew for an absolute fact that I was not going to be employed by this gym very long.

People were treated terribly. Both client and employee. Being moved around like pawns in a game of chess. Practicing and duplicating nationwide procedures that focused, not on client's results, but on the game of numbers it took to make a gym run. The game of numbers it took to strip money away from hard-working people, regardless of what the client decided to do for her or himself. I also learned, most of the managers were not people-people... rather, really good at playing the numbers to sell product. I never saw proactive steps taken towards solutions; I instead saw a whole lot of reacting to problems, which could have been avoided.

I became a master closer, but I did not want to use this power for evil. I was moving product left and right and it had zero to do with gym procedure. Most of my clients in my roster had been exposed to the gym's product, some for years, and absolutely did not like it, regardless of what trainer was placed in front of them.

My success had to do with results. How clients were being treated and listened to. The monthly cost and agreement no longer mattered to them. I was not selling the procedure that was being sold by the gym. I was selling myself and my story. Sharing my vision for them to create their own. Pair this with believing in people and you have a product without a price tag.

# CHAPTER 7

## DO I WANT TO LEAVE THE CORPORATE ENVIRONMENT?

## "WHEN YOU SAY YOU ARE GOING TO DO SOMETHING AND THEN DO IT, YOU WILL BE SUCCESSFUL... UNTIL THEN, YOU ARE JUST SAYING SOMETHING."

You are in the mega gym and you ask yourself... Do I want to be here any longer, doing things the "gym" way, rather than doing things "my" way? Can I put up with this monotonous love and hate relationship from my managers? Can I take my training to the next step? If you are asking yourself these questions, you should already be taking active steps to leave. You see potential in yourself that others may not see. Since the only opinion that really matters is yours, I guess you better start packing!

If you are getting results for your clients, your clients are no longer concerned with your gym, I promise you. You have created a friend. Multiple friends. At this point, you have a core group of clientele. People who will follow you no matter where you go and no matter how long you may ever be absent from them. When you change someone's life on a level based upon the capabilities of this industry, you cannot be matched. There is no price that can be placed on YOUR value. Anytime value is placed over price, you create a sale. You create an idea to be believed in.

You always have clients who come and go. Someone moves. Another trainer was sick. Someone had to leave early that day. A friend of a client wants to try you out. It happens. But your core will always exist. 5, 10, 20, 100..

You have made the decision to leave, but someone has signed an agreement for training. Luckily, the hassle is dwindling because most gyms do not even offer agreements anymore. Just about all systems are month to month now. Take note that I am not saying contract. I am saying agreement. People are almost pushed into thinking they are signing a contract with huge penalties if they wish to opt out. Be sure to check your paperwork, but in most cases, all you have signed is a form, acknowledging the gym to debit a certain amount of money from your account every month. Neither your social security number or credit is affected. Nor can it be sent to collections. The truth is, the industry has such a bad name, that regulations are stacked against the corporate gym "agreement." Not to say the structure cannot be fixed. It can. And a lot of gyms are now taking steps to fix it.

There were many cases when a client would have a moving concern. In the city I was training clients, there were not many residents around. Our clients were before work, during lunch, and after work. Duh Jason... that is the schedule at every gym. No, I mean, we were right in the middle of corporate America. The heartbeat of blue and white collar. The city people would travel to, from their outlying suburb. If it wasn't a business, it was an apartment. If you wanted a home... you had to travel a few miles. We had many clients who relocated from place to place as often as some people buy their supplements.

"What if I move to a city where this gym doesn't exist?"

We were trained to tell the client how to get out of the agreement. Simply turn off your debit/credit card. When the gym calls you, tell them to leave you alone. There is not much else that can be done. I am not saying this is the best thing to do in all situations. Communication is key, always. This is just what we were taught to do at my gym.

More than 2/3rds of my clients tried to go to management in order to see a proper way out of their agreements, however, the management at my gym was often unreliable and offered little help. This was one of my many reasons for leaving. I am not condoning turning off your card. Just be aware of your rights as a consumer.

When I left my gym, I walked out with my core group, which was close to 15 clients. It did not matter how I felt about my gym personally. It did not matter the faults I saw in the system. It didn't matter that people could have done a more passionate job. What mattered was, if I wanted to move further along and take the next step I needed to take in my life, I needed to leave this gym. And my clients needed to come with me.

Above all, these people are people, and they belong to no one. They should be able to freely make a decision to leave, especially if they are dissatisfied. An agreement is put in place to replace the relationship of trust. That way, if a client is not happy; if the client has lost trust in the company, they are stuck making a decision to either put up with it or lose their money. And that isn't right. If you feel you are a big part of these people's lives, you have a responsibility to tell them you are leaving. And if you are trained on how to get a person out of the situation, you have an even bigger responsibility to be honest with them so they do not lose more money.

All of these people signed new agreements because of their trust in me. Never because I asked them to. I owed them this knowledge.

This may sound redirected or funny, but you SHOULD take some time to work in a corporate gym. If you started out on your own and built a business to the level of success you wanted to, without this advice, wonderful! That is even better. However, being in this big box allowed me to work with hundreds of people and learn whom I should and should not work with, exactly what skills I possessed, and what I could bring to the table. It also taught me, the corporate gym was exactly where I did not want to be. That was a very valuable lesson because the variables which did not satisfy me, pushed me out the door even quicker.

Your greatest strengths are your greatest weaknesses. We always want to amplify our strengths. New surprises give you a chance to face your fears and weaknesses. Embrace new scenarios, new problems, new questions, and harder personalities to figure out. This is what allows us to grow. Expand your mind and horizons as much as you can and get to know as many people as you can throughout your career.

## CHAPTER 8

## BENEFITS OF A BIG BOX GYM: SCIENCE THAT WILL FOLLOW YOU, NO MATTER WHERE YOU GO.

## "SCIENCE, COMES FROM THE LATIN WORD – SCIENTIA – WHICH MEANS, TO KNOW THY SELF."

Before I go on to the next section, I want to take a moment to talk about some of the core benefits I learned while working in gyms. I don't want it to seem as though I am bashing the corporate environment, because I got my start there too. And it was a necessary starting point, for me at least.

Halfway through my training career, I started working at a more intimate gym; smaller, less clientele and everyone knew everyone and their children by first name basis. It was such a great, positive environment, after my transition into self-employment. I was able to take my Emma to work with me, who was 3 at the time. I also had the opportunity to work alongside some of the greatest trainers and athletes in the industry. However, most, if not all of these trainers, all had their background in the corporate environment. They paid their dues and earned their stripes. There may have been a few that started on their own, and they are more awesome for it... however, you will have more opportunities to learn from and more people you will be surrounded by, that will shape you into trainer you strive to be, with a start at corporate. Even more beneficial to your growth, is the ability to make mistakes and learn from them while you are still learning the ropes.

Let's face it; once you get out on your own, there will be a higher expectation of your abilities. There will be a higher expectation of your communication skills and your ability to lead other people. There will be a higher expectation of trust, and more value will be expected from you also. You better be able to deliver. Here are some key elements to success that will follow you outside of the gym, and no matter where you take your career. Even if you leave the training industry you will be able to adapt the same methodology and principles.

## People, People, and More People

Diversity among us is so beautiful. We spend so much time as a society looking at everyone's differences. Our individuality makes us unique amongst one another and I believe our likeness can draw us closer together as a people.

Unfortunately, we live in a society of people who take. We love our things and use people when we should be using our things and loving people. I was coasting through a social media page and I read a quote from an unknown author. It read:

**"Welcome to our society. You will be judged on what you wear, what music you listen to, what you look like, how you act, who you hang out with, and on practically every other personal trait and imperfection you have. And you will be made fun of, just for being who you are. Enjoy your stay." – unknown**

As a person having weighed close to 400 pounds, I remember being afraid of going to the gym. I remember the feeling of everyone judging me and feeling like an outcast. There were times where I wanted to quit before I ever got started because of the amount of people who were going to be in the gym that day.

I even remember buying a bicycle to ride to the gym. The first dozen or so times I rode it, I had to work my way up to making it to the gym; which was 3.5 miles away. The night after my first "long ride," I cried myself to sleep because I was in so much pain. I did not remember bicycling being so hard when I was younger. (How had I allowed myself to get to this point?) The first 4 times I finally made it to the door, I turned back around and rode home because I was so tired and didn't want to feel embarrassed as I struggled through my workout. I did not have the energy to explain to everyone that I felt lazy and miserable because I forgotten how to ride a bike.

But I kept at it. I kept at it because I found a trainer. Tim. I was down to about 335 pounds by the time I began training with Tim. He taught me to focus on the workout. Focus on change and results will come. Don't focus on results because it will just frustrate you. He also taught me that no one cared that I was in the gym. My fears about everyone staring at me were all in my head. And everyone else in the gym had the exact same fear, regardless of fitness level.

Later I would learn about energy and how we all create the feeling of isolation in a corporate gym, with our hearts and minds. Think about it; if every single person who walks into the gym is thinking to themselves – I just want to be left alone – I hope no one is looking at me – I want to hurry and get out of here – it would only make sense that the building turns into a cesspool of isolationists. The dome of introversion is introduced by the very hearts of the people in attendance.

Your job as a trainer is to be there for your client. You are a personal trainer. You are a teacher, a leader, a mentor, a therapist... the list goes on and on. I remember instances of female clients who were afraid to travel to certain parts of the gym because of past rude gestures and/or advances from ego-driven males in the gym. And I always took charge and made sure their comfort was my number one priority. I remember at least half a dozen occasions when I had some of these very same ego-driven males in my face. Some of them could have very well pounded me into the ground. But I always stood my ground. I never raised my voice, never got out of control, or stooped to their level. I adopted the idea of "kill them with kindness."

If you are watching 2 people shout at one another, you may think to yourself, those people are crazy. If you see one person shouting while the other remains calm, you will have an easier time discerning who may be the one provoking the quarrel. It was also very nice to receive compliments on how I was able to keep my cool.

Passion drives results. Results drive passion. It is a continuous cycle. I remember taking my first before picture. I was about 340 pounds. There are almost no pictures of me available at my heaviest because of my self-esteem at the time. To this day, I am not quite sure how my future would have progressed through this major shift in my life had I not taken that first picture. I took another picture a month later. And another a month later. Almost always 30 days apart, give or take a couple days.

At one point, I started losing hope. I began feeling defeated. I was 2 weeks into my first plateau and I felt lost. I made the mistake, at first, of stepping on the scale every single day. I had not yet developed enough knowledge in the beginning to know that not only did your weight fluctuate; it was also meaningless if you were not putting it side by side with your body-fat percentage. I was following BMI and weighing in at different times of the day. There was never any consistency, but there were those pictures.

I uploaded them from my cell phone to my computer and I could faintly see the thumbnails. I noticed a drastic change. I saw results. My entire body had changed completely! I was ecstatic, and I wanted to share this feeling with everyone and let them experience it for themselves.

One of the biggest reasons why we plateau as beginners is because of lack of knowledge. We know nothing about form. We know nothing about regimented eating. We know absolutely nothing about supplements. We read magazines and we get our advice from "they said" and "bro" science. We often ask advice from people who are not in shape and have never been in shape; or maybe they tried a fad diet and lost 30 pounds, so we feel they are somewhat of an expert in our eyes. They give us bad advice and we willingly follow it. We fill our fridge full of foods that we will never eat and will eventually trash. And we will have a pantry full of supplements, with no knowledge of when to take them or how they really work.

This is the reason we hire nutritionists and trainers. Trainers take us away from "they said" science. We finally learn to stop doing so much cardio and stop restricting our calories. We learn to focus on building muscle. We are taught the importance of form and protein. And as trainers, you should over exaggerate form to no end. Sure, our bodies have the ability to become stronger every single time we lift weights, but are we really growing the muscles we intended to grow? As a trainer, are you making sure your clients are always in correct posture, with their specific postural deviations, injuries, or ailments in mind?

The reason for a plateau is because we aren't doing anything to overcome what we did before. We get stuck in a routine. I remember going to each and every machine and doing 3 sets of 12 and having no clue why I was doing 3 sets of 12. I am sure it was because "they" said it, or I read it in a magazine.

Something that later occurred to me… in my early twenties, I took interest in being a text broker for a little while. I did not try it for very long and never really made any money doing it. I worked for an online publisher that would post assignments. These assignments or tasks were in the form of magazine and newspaper publications. You had various tasks from book writers with multiple pen names, using "ghost writers" to write books about generic tasks in order to benefit from other streams of passive income.

You had to take a few tests, so they could assess your skills as a writer, editor, and proofreader. I scored in the top of all available categories. Compensation per word was the payout, and I can't for the life of me remember how much it was, but low and behold, I never felt passion for writing about other people's ideas. Of the available jobs, most were magazine articles. Quite a few were articles written about weight-loss, weight management, diets, fitness, how-to articles, instructions, and tips. The point is, actual experts in the field were writing zero of these publications; very good writers, with little to no knowledge of consequence, were writing them.

Lack of knowledge kills passion. It can force someone to give up on their goal if they aren't careful. It is your job as a trainer to know and believe in, without a doubt, every word that comes out of your mouth. It is your job as a client, to find a trainer who is knowledgeable and not only cares about your results, but has a past history of recreating these results.

One of my biggest plateaus in my weight-loss journey was once I became a trainer. I was about 250 pounds. In my mind, I was at the peak of fitness. I forgot what drove me to ride my bike uphill on the way to the gym to kick my own ass, then enjoy the fruits of my labor as I coasted downhill on the way home. In Georgia, it was the exact opposite. Downhill on the way to the gym, and after a brutal gym session, I had to cover an 800ft positive elevation change in the span of 2 miles. I forgot what it was like to be the student, and for a few months, I acquired this title of teacher and master trainer and just stopped progressing. I let my very own victory defeat me and cloud my judgment on how I ate and how I worked out. I stopped pushing myself.

I began doing a program with my very own version of "3 sets of 12." There was no plan to my training regimen. No thought behind it. I was so focused on my client's goals that I forgot all about myself. I eventually lost passion for my own push. There was nothing written on paper… no plan. It was later, when I joined the smaller and more intimate gym, that I learned our passion is constant. It is we the people who are flaky. We give up on our goals. Not passion. Passion is always around the corner, waiting to be put into good use.

I could very well apply these questions to any plateau in my life. Relationships, friendships, careers, health… it is so devastating and frustrating, but you still must ask yourself, how can I get past this? What am I doing wrong? What can I do better?

As trainers, we are so often blamed for a client's plateau. As a client, I realized I needed to take responsibility for myself. My battles were mine and I didn't need to blame someone's regimen for my weight gain or lack of muscle gain. If you are not training for anything, you are exercising for nothing. There must always be a goal in mind. You cannot expect your coach to hold you accountable if you are unwilling to hold yourself accountable.

We all like to eat our favorite foods. We must take a moment to realize it is only conditioning though. Imagine when you were a child… Your parents told you to finish everything on your plate. You were told stories of children in other countries who were starving, all because you weren't finishing your spaghetti. Or, you think of celebratory moments of nostalgia, like a birthday, or Christmas party... or even those painful moments of loss where a dear friend or family member was taken; or a relationship ended and you dive into binge eating. There is so much life that happens, but you can't overeat every single time it does. I learned this the hard way. It isn't so much the food we crave, as it is the ideas, feelings, thoughts, and emotions we attach to the food we are craving, and therefore, overeating.

Being at the smaller gym, I was able to create group classes where I actually worked out with my classes rather than just training them. I had morning and evening classes and we were able to work up massive amounts of sweat and results together. I dropped the title of teacher and became a student again. I needed to take heed and humble myself in my new environment of professionals. I realized although I had gained so much knowledge, there was still so much more to absorb and learn. My clients' mistakes became my mistakes. My clients' results became my results. I became my own client.

Now that you have taken responsibility, you need to make a physical or even a mental list of what you feel you can improve upon and what you feel is holding you back. The reality of it is, you just need to work harder. That's it! It could upset a few people that I say that, but it is the simple truth. I left the corporate gym, had heart surgery, then started working like a mad man 2 months before I was cleared to work out, and became a lean and mean 215 pounds within a couple of months. I took my life into my own hands again.

There are 168 hours in the week. I can almost guarantee if you apply a little bit more time into what it is you are doing to reach your goal, you will get there faster. If there are 7 days in a week, you need to be working harder for more of those days. Take a shot at consistent efforts rather than doing a whole lot one day, and completely skipping the next.

What are you doing when you are in the gym? Are you working your butt off? Are you, "no paining no gaining?" There are two kinds of pain. There is the pain where your muscles hurt. You feel so tired and fatigued and you feel you had a pretty good workout. And then there are times when your central nervous system is damaged and you know to your core, since you cannot properly use your limbs, your workout was effective and results will be achieved. You create that famous mind-muscle connection. You almost feel as though you left a part of your soul in the gym. That isn't tough talk. That is talk from someone who lost 200 pounds of body fat and gained 25 pounds of muscle in 2 years. I have lived the pain.

Most importantly, we need to stop looking for reasons and people to blame. If you are a trainer and you want more clients or wish to move on to a better avenue because you feel stuck, go! Flee! Move on, or work harder. If you are a client, don't blame your trainer. Your trainer is the one person who is definitively on your team. Even when you are being fed negativity from your friends and family. Every time you blame someone, you are pushing yourself further into giving up. You will eventually build up so much negativity in your mind, you will lose your passion and drive, and you may altogether lose interest.

Whatever your plateau is… your job, your relationships, your weight loss; you can take out a piece of paper and start drawing out dots to connect. But you really only need to draw one dot. Yourself.

Being in the corporate gym, I also got to reap the benefits of a steady paycheck. I was able to build up a schedule of clients that I did not have to work for. The clients kept coming. My reputation was helping of course, and I stayed booked solid. But, I was grinding away and still making the same wage as everyone else. Just working more hours. And of course, that steady paycheck was based on a smaller idea of thinking. I know for a fact that there are some managers of some gyms making upwards of six figures a year. I did not want to be a gym manager though. I did not want to live the stressful life of working 100 hours a week and being owned by a corporation. At the time, I wanted to be a trainer. I wanted to work on my own leadership skills. I had no interest in being a top-hat. Ask yourself the same question… Do you see yourself being a gym manager? Or did you come here to launch a training career?

I mentioned earlier, I was able to work with people I would not normally work with. We are always so quick to jump on the athlete who can take in all of our skills as a trainer, but being in the gym gives you the opportunity to work with all walks of life. The more challenging clients will make you a stronger trainer.

The smaller gym I worked in had a higher expectation of trainer. So there was a higher expectation of client. There were things I was just unable to teach any new trainers who wanted to join my team, but had no corporate gym experience. I usually showed them the ropes for a few weeks, told them the "ins and outs" and expectations of the corporate gym, and then urged them to seek temporary employment in one.

Don't get yourself into anything you really aren't sure you can commit to. Are you really going to wake up at 5am? Can you really fit in that early morning boot camp 4 days a week? At least being in the box, you can make a few mistakes. I was punctual with every client, but at the same time, people do make mistakes. It is a little bit easier to send a text or make a phone call for a no show, or even for your client to do the same when being employed. Once you are on your own, you could very well lose your client for lack of results or punctuality.

Know the role you wish to play in the gym. Everyone's job is necessary, from front desk personnel, to beginner trainer or veteran trainer, old or up and coming manager, or any of the above that are tired of the system, and ready to take on the real world with open arms.

# CHAPTER 9

# NOW YOU ARE ON YOUR OWN

# "YOUR SUCCESS DEPENDS SOLELY UPON THE SECOND LETTER IN SUCCESS."

**Any numbers used here are for example purposes only. Your ultimate results and success are up to you and your own level of awesomeness.**

Where are you going to train your clients? You should have been ready for this. You have fired your boss. Or maybe someone caught wind to your wanting to leave and you were then asked to leave.

With no venue? What about that training studio that wants 60% of your income?

Get out there… get creative. Make relationships. Start talking to people. There are apartment complexes looking for personal trainers so they can add YOU to their list of amenities. Some of these apartments will even give you discounted rent to live on site.

There are people out there who own small studios who care more about helping people and building a reputation than taking all of your money.

There are, my personal favorite, local recreation centers. And from what I have seen, no matter what city you may live in, these are absolutely free. Follow the rules and guidelines. Do a little bit of community service for your city. You will become a bigger presence than you originally thought imaginable, just because you will be positioning yourself to help promote change in an entire community, by deciding to work out your clients here.

Set a price and have everyone pay you the same fee, or close to it. And have everyone pay you on the same day. The 1$^{st}$ sounds good. Sure, you can keep a schedule and charge everyone different rates. They even have software programs that will help you keep track of it all. But, why?

If you are charging Person A, this amount, and Person B is doing this program, and paying you on this day, but Person C wants to do this, and also wants… Yuck!! Stop trying to nickel and dime people. Put a price on the value you wish to offer and do not change it. Do not discount it or offer specials. Discounting your price is discounting your self-worth. Set 1 price. Paid on 1 day. I called it rent. Rent is due. That way, you can focus on results and get back to business. Get used to the idea of long money, rather than quick money.

For example… You have 10 clients paying you 300 dollars per month. Some of them are seeing you twice a week, some are seeing you four times a week. An average is still your best bet. Who cares what who is doing. Make it easy on yourself and your clients. Not to mention, the last thing you want is for a client to find out they are paying more than another client for equal service. If someone starts in the middle of the month, pro-rate it and move on.

Next, consolidation of time is a huge key in business. There is no reason why it should not be applied here too. Creating synergy between your clients is a must. I learned this from the pros. Grouping people together and creating a team environment from the first moment you can, will pay off a thousand fold.

Everyone is missing something. Which is a very big reason why they are working with you to begin with. I enjoyed taking different personalities and grouping them together with like-minded individuals to create a "complete person," so to speak. Then you take that group and pair them alongside another group and you not only create a team, you create an unstoppable force. You can create a following of leaders and health enthusiasts just like yourself.

Some of these people did not work well with others. They would be placed in another group, or I would still train them individually. Group training was my primary focus now, so individual clients had to fit where they could fit. Think about your income potential and time potential. Simply introducing people, and creating trust and friendships, can maximize your income potential just by your being the common buffer of everyone involved.

So let us do some simple math. Remember, these results aren't typical, and some will do a whole lot better than this… this is a mere example to follow.

You left the corporate gym. You have your 10 clients, but you know you are now going to pick up the pace for more business. You are going to market, you are going to advertise, you are going to push. You want 30 clients and no one can stop you. You know what it is going to take to get those 30 clients, so get to work.

You have your 10 clients paying you $3,000 a month and they are taking up 30 hours a week of your time, regardless of how they are scheduled. That means, when you get to 30 clients, you will only be working 90 hours a week. Wait… What? 90 hours a week? Please keep in mind, we all have the same amount of time in a day.

Group these people together. When I say group, I

do not mean boot camp. We will go over boot camps later, but when I think of group training, I think of a gym setting. Lots of weights, lots of dumbbells. Maybe even a chalk or dry erase board with a list of tasks to do. When I think of a boot camp, I think of an outdoor class. Usually used for fun or conditioning. Calisthenics and bodyweight exercises with "time" being the focus. Group training is for building strength and power in the body and mind and building team rapport. A boot camp is a place to have fun with the people from the groups; using games and thinking outside of the box to create a fun environment, rather than a working environment.

I digress. This example was actually taught to me when I began working in my first studio gym. Take your original 10, charge them $250 dollars a month to do a group workout and schedule it 3 nights per week. But, $250 per month per client is less money. Really? Because it seems to me you just condensed 30 hours down into 3. Which means, your next group of 10 will put you at 6 total hours. The next group of 10 will put you at 9 hours, and so on.

Create specific groups and specific class times so that your clients always know when they are supposed to be there. If your client wants to try out another group, give them the freedom to do so.

Charging a lower price will incentivize the client to try the group workout. Lead with your best ability to create an environment, which will make them never want to go back to individual training. Find your leaders in your groups and delegate responsibilities, not tasks, which will not only allow your leaders to grow, but your new people will have multiple team members to put their faith into. It may be cool to be the one in charge… but it is even cooler to create and be amongst leaders who believe in your ability to lead them too.

Remember to cater to individual needs. This is why you need to build a core group of leaders rather than taking on the task yourself. On day number one of becoming a trainer, you should have learned about visual, audial, and kinesthetic learning types. You will have people who are great at taking direction, people who are great at being hands on, and people who are great at watching someone else do it. Be sure you have people in your groups who have primary strengths in each of these behaviors.

3 groups of 10, at 3 hours a week , for $250 a piece every month. That comes to $7,500 dollars per month for 36 hours of your time. And all the extra time in the world for individuals who do not want to do group training. There is not a single corporate gym out there willing to pay you $7,500 per month for 9 hours a week of work. There is no amount of 1 on 1 sessions you can do in that same amount of time, which provide value at least, and make that kind of income.

If you want to go out of town or take a few days off… or maybe you just aren't feeling well one night, or your child is sick. Now you have a group of leaders who can run the show without you around, rather than having to make a choice to not get paid or pay another trainer. They are committed to results, your programming, and your way of running the show. A huge underlying factor they sought out when they started with you, accountability, still exists within a group.

Since I am doing this in a gym, what if another trainer tries to steal my business because I took a day off? Then I am afraid you are going about your business the wrong way. If you are afraid of someone stealing your business, you do not know how to run your business. If you have a fear of loss, it is caused by the doubt you have created in your mind of a fault you have in your own system or own self. Rather than worrying, take the time to educate yourself OUT of this fear. Take the time to create a program that will keep people from never thinking about another trainer, again. You have the ability. You have the value. Get on it.

# CHAPTER 10

## GROUP TRAINING VS. BOOT CAMPS

## "THE OPPOSITE OF GIVING IS GIVING MORE."

Some trainers may completely disagree with me on this section, depending on how their business is set up. This was my experience on my journey. Some people may have a ridiculous marketing program, and they could have started out creating a multi-million dollar boot camp training company by taking the exact opposite action. And if they wrote a book explaining steps and processes to help you, that is even better! Buy it too! Learn everything you can from every single person you can. Take the time to visit other trainer's classes too. It helped me, a lot.

There is a huge difference between these two methods of training. Boot camps and (in the gym) group training. If you do not feel this is true, you should consider adopting this perspective. Not only should there be a difference to you as a trainer, there should definitely be a difference in methods to the client. You should also help create an even bigger belief and perception in the two. A client SHOULD know that a difference exists.

Why? If you are building your name, building your business, becoming the greatest trainer with the biggest reach you can possibly have, you should be doing boot camps for free. I know some of you may kick me in the butt for saying that... but it is true. Business is not about products. It is about relationships with people and the vision you create for others, about yourself and your business.

I have been fascinated for years that we will follow the laws of man, but not the laws of the universe. No matter what you believe in, laws of prosperity, generosity, and balance exist that only we can take the time to understand. I too, followed this behavior pattern for quite some time. Which is why I vowed to spend my life educating people out of this limiting behavior once I came to realize I too, was trapped.

The Law of Compensation states we are rewarded in direct proportion to the amount of value placed upon the service we have provided to other people... to the world or universe overall. Work, in the general sense of the word, is not service. Service is the gift or gifts you have within you that you can share with the world. Money is the reward for your service. Directly correlated to the amount of value placed in the service being performed. If you want to raise your compensation, raise the level of value being placed on your contribution to mankind. If you are broke, you are not adding enough value to enough people. If you want to become wealthy, provide more value to more people. If you want to become wealthy overnight, provide more value to more people overnight.

The universe is always in balance and will give you what you have worked your ass off for, and what you deserve. Not necessarily what you think you deserve. We only receive, because of who we are, not because of what we may or may not want.

Boot camps should be seldom and they should be free because of two things; service and value. You can immediately provide service to a large number of people, and add even more value to yourself by providing this service for free. And since you have tripled your income by now and you have condensed your schedule down to less than 10 hours per week, you can definitely provide this service for free.

Do not think for a second that you must wait until you have started earning $10,000 a month and working the schedule of your dreams to start providing free classes. Remember the law of compensation. You are actually being rewarded with a higher income because you took the time and effort to provide free services when you did not have the money to do so. You tithe when you go to church. Think of this in the same manner. You are adding more value, with an even larger contribution.

People make a buying decision based on trade. Is the service you are offering worth more to me than the amount of currency I have to spend? If so, I will buy your product. So the more value you add to your service, the easier your client or potential client's decision is to make a trade with you.

Let me further break down how you can benefit from running free boot camps because I know some of you may still have some questions.

You have all of your group sessions on varying days throughout the week. Pick a night during the week where you provide a free outdoor class. And you can blast these classes on social media as well as having your group classes know they must attend these classes too. It is also their responsibility to bring new members to the boot camp and blast it on their social media outlets too.

You will be an even bigger success because of your realization of relationships and business. Since you are a personal trainer, you should be focused on a personal relationship and building more personal relationships with more of the people your clients interact with on a personal level. Word of mouth awesome... excessive "non-stop of the mouth," because someone cannot get enough of you, is even better!

Say you tried to pick some number out of thin air to charge for a boot camp... how are you going to price it for your clients? For guests? What about the guest that periodically shows up? The one-timers? There are way too many variables to get in your way because these are indeed completely separate types of classes. Completely separate ideas.

Now you have created an outlet for guests. For friends that want to try out your program. For spouses who couldn't make the time before, simply because they were busy working, or even watching the kids. Not only that, but the kids can come too!

I remember one of my clients on the phone saying to a friend, "Hey, you have been asking about my results and I told you I have this cool ass trainer! Well, now he is putting on free classes so you better be here!"

Have contests, with rewards for the person who brings the most guests to a boot camp. Take fieldtrips to grocery stores and blast it all over your social media outlets. Teach clients, neighbors, and absolute strangers how to shop. How to read nutrition labels to make better decisions at the store. Do all of this for free too. Put on free seminars or classes to teach people squat mechanics, or how sugar affects major body systems.

One of my favorite activities to build rapport I used on countless occasions, I would have clients over for dinner and prepare a good hearty, healthy meal for them. This would teach them to cook healthier meals for their families, and we would all have more intimate time to get to know one another.

Again, by doing something so simple for free, you will create an opportunity for new people to see what you are all about. On top of that, you open yourself up for more exposure in your local community by taking these simple steps. I picked up clientele in grocery stores, restaurants, going out for runs… received ideas on growth from attending other local trainer's boot camps and made great friends. All because, I genuinely wanted to help people and was recognized for it.

Most importantly, I have been blessed with the opportunity to meet and help many new faces. Free or not, the man with the marker makes the money. Get your face in front of more people. Concentrate on making the long buck by planting really good seeds. Not making a nickel and dime again and again. A new attitude towards your business venture is one of many actions you will take that the other guy isn't willing to do.

Think of the amount of potential personal training clients you will have, who already know and love you. Seeing results from a program you are putting on for them, and not charging a dime for it. Turn your reach into gold by helping more people.

If you wake up in the morning and ask yourself, "How much money can I make today?" – your results will differ far greater than someone waking up asking, "How many people can I help today?"

Do not limit your own success in business. The universe will take care of you if you allow it to. Add value to your program. Value is results. Value is being on time. Value is not arguing with clients. Value is being willing to be wrong. Value is not expecting monetary compensation for every move you make. Value is having confidence in your ability to lead.

If someone wants to go workout with another trainer for a little while, let them go. You know they will come back. Do not downplay the other trainer to make yourself look better. This will only make you look weaker. Rave about their strengths. Make them look like a hero. I promise, this will in turn make you look the hero. That other trainer may not have the value you have. There is no way they can provide the service you are willing to provide. Or, maybe they can. This may be a test. It may be time for you to step it up. If you want your name known, make sure every person you come in contact with has zero need to ever contact another personal trainer.

Your client, working with another trainer, can only benefit you. You may catch wind of new ideas you can then apply to your own program. You can network and get to know fellow trainers so you can both exchange ideals and exemplify both of your strengths. One thing I told every one of my clients; if I could do my weight-loss all over again, I would work with multiple trainers rather than sticking to just one. Tim and I worked magically together, however, this did limit my knowledge when I first entered the field myself. Not every client can be worked with the exact same way. I had to learn this on my own.

If you KNOW you are effective, if you KNOW you add unmatched value, if you KNOW you can get results, if you KNOW you have a great product; your business will thrive. You should never have to beg anyone to become or remain a client. Do not conform. Do not keep clients who make you unhappy or stress you out, just because you think you need their money. You don't. YOU are worth more than that. Believe it.

# CHAPTER 11

## CREATE A SOCIAL MEDIA MOVEMENT

## "THERE ARE NO COINCIDENCES. ONLY OPPORTUNITIES THAT CAN SET YOUR LIFE ON A COMPLETELY DIFFERENT COURSE. AND THOUGHTS AND FEARS THAT CAN KILL THOSE OPPORTUNITIES."

Social media can be your best friend or your worst enemy depending on how you perceive yourself and whom you portray yourself to be online. Anytime you post anything online, the whole world can see it. That doesn't mean the whole world is seeing it. It is up to you to take some steps to help them find it.

I want to start this by saying, your influence on social media has NOTHING to do with your abilities as a trainer or leader. If anything, it is a simple reflection of how well you market yourself online and/or "how long" you have been marketing yourself online.

DO NOT ever post anything online that you don't mind being around FOREVER. No one cares about your fights, your breakups, and your passive aggressive remarks, directed towards a waitress, that pissed you off. If you are looking for negative attention, you will surely find it. Shit happens to all of us, but we are in full control of how we react to it and allow it to affect us. If you can't keep your cool, it speaks volumes of your character. It isn't so much about what you are posting as much as it is about you as a person, or the intent behind your post. A good person will only say good things. Plain and simple. If someone attacks you, and others do in fact believe it, you did not need those people in your life anyway. Remain positive.

It wasn't until 2012 when I finally decided to join the online movement. I was already halfway done with my training career before I ever started broadcasting myself online through posts, blogs, comments, or videos. I did, however, make a promise to myself to always remain as positive, professional, and as motivating as possible. If I was going to make a post, I was going to make a difference. I wasn't going to repost other people's philosophy, I was going to create my own. I wasn't going to post hate. I was going to post love.

A general rule of thumb is to not post for sheer entertainment. In the time you have been online, you have created a following. And those people are your audience. You need to make posts for your audience. You are NOT your audience, so cater to their needs, if that is your purpose. Change their life. If you are sharing and posting everything you think is entertaining, you will not get as far as you would like to. If you overload your audience with BS or negativity, it will only be a matter of time before you lose your audience.

I like using tags. A good friend of mine, and fellow trainer, told me she loved to be tagged in posts because it showed her that she was being thought of. She mentioned that it speaks volumes about the person tagged more so than the meaning behind the actual post. When you tag someone, it appears on his or her feed too, not just your own. This way, everyone they know can see it as well.

In the beginning, I made an agreement with a large number of people on my friends list, granting me permission to tag them in photos. This way, many can see a post rather than a mere few. Just be careful who you tag and do not tag. Do not offend people. You should not be tagging the same people anyway. Not everyone can remind you of every post, and everyone will not relate to one post in a special manner.

I tag specific people in workout posts, a different

group of people in motivational posts, and any posts I make about relationships or for the ladies, I have a separate group of people for those as well. Make sure you are tagging and posting, in general, for a purpose. Tag with meaning. A simple post can go from catching the attention of 2 people, to 100 people, or even 1,000 people. A post can mean 10 new followers and a few potential clients. At the same time, one post can cause you to lose half of your fan base, or show the world who you really are as a person. A fake person has an image to maintain. A real person doesn't.

Stop posting pictures of yourself all of the time. Stop. Yes, you are a trainer with a nice body, so make yourself a separate page for your modeling career. If you want more clients, you should be posting pictures of your existing clients and celebrating their milestones, victories and successes, rather than your own.

Stop posting pictures of the mountains of supplements you are experimenting with. To the average person, all of that stuff will only give them expensive pee. And the average magazine reader will see your picture and think they can fill their bloodstream with all of those supplements and achieve the same result as you. I did, before I was a trainer. You are creating an idea in someone's head that can cause them more harm than good.

Do not over-post. 2 to 3 posts per day are far more effective than a post at 6am, 9am, 12pm, 12:25pm, 2pm, 5pm, 7pm... 9am and 6pm are prime times. Selective posts are more effective than over-posting. Over-posting will sometimes cause the algorithms of some sites to make sure your posts are never seen, in attempt to reduce spam.

Start joining "groups" of people online so you have more outlets to get your message across. Stay away from personal training groups. Seriously. How are you going to pick up new clientele in a group full of other trainers? You need single moms, college kids, and "Average-Joes." It may sound funny, but you are more likely to find new clients in a garage sale group than a personal training group. Unless you are looking to network and grab up a few more trainers for your expanding personal training business, go after "real" people.

Every trainer has a philosophy in which they believe in. Never find yourself in a dispute with someone who feels they know more than you. You too may end up looking the fool. Any attention is good attention, so ignore them and move on.

Use video outlets too. Pick up a camera as often as you can. I cannot stress how important this is with the push of online training programs, coupled with the abundance of free information that is available online. You are smart. Get that knowledge out there. Knowledge is free. How we apply it to our lives and share it with others, gives it value.

Workout videos, video blogs, free nutrition information, boot camp and group class commercials, these can all make your business grow. There is no end to the possibilities, as I only listed very few examples. I know you must have a head full of ideas you wish to share with the world.

Take note: you do not have to broadcast yourself, but this will give more people an opportunity to see you. How do you get more views? Make more content. If you are going to spend the time creating an online presence or following, you may as well go as big as you possibly can and create a movement.

# CHAPTER 12

## MLM – MULTI LEVEL OR NETWORK-MARKETING

### "BUSINESS IS ABOUT RELATIONSHIPS, NOT SELLING STUFF. BECOME A PROFESSIONAL BEST FRIEND AND MARKET YOURSELF."

This is your "risk vs. reward" section. It was mine too. I never imagined my life turning this direction... from pool man, to trainer, to speaker, to now a master student in MLM... traveling the country and teaching people how to generate wealth with such a cool process and way of thinking. I love to speak.

That was my vision. To travel and speak with and get to know people for a living. However, speaking is a service I offer. Of course I would not mind someone paying to hear me talk. After all, we are in business to make money. I would just use the proceeds to help more children and more people, anyway. I would rather speak and share my knowledge for free. But, if this is the path I am choosing, giving so much for free, how am I to get compensated? If the man with the marker makes the money, how am I going to make money?

MLM is a job. A job that can be performed like the mail boy that no one knows or the CEO that everyone wants to know. Your success in MLM comes from the amount of success you want to have in MLM. Your doubts of failure in MLM probably come from someone else's ideas about it. Well, isn't that messed up?

I know by now you have already doubled or tripled your income because you have been following my advice thus far. Or maybe you wish to apply this chapter to your business before you ever get started training. I wish I had. Up until now though, you still have one asset... yourself. You may have a few more if you already have other trainers out there working for you. But what happens if the clientele dries up? What happens if one of your trainers walks and takes their beloved clients with them? What happens if you get sick or injured and can't go to work for a couple of weeks?

A lot of trainers, including myself, were skeptical

of MLM. Having no money and being skeptical is a very bad way to live. I used to absolutely trash talk any kind of nutrition company in the multi-level marketing field. To me, the message was just wrong. At the time, they did not represent the morals or ethics I would be willing to call my own. Clients are not supposed to have an abundance of nutrition knowledge. This is why they are taking the time to come to you. If one of my clients were to ask any expanded information about any supplementation, sure, I was always more than happy to give advice. But I was never going to take a catalog with 500 products and slap it on a table in front of a client, with expectations of becoming rich off of the ignorance of the very lives I helped to grow and change.

On the flip side, being a fitness professional, everyone asked my advice on nutritional information, supplements, vitamins, types of diets, etc. It is the name of the game and the business you and I both signed up for. All I ask is that you don't confuse clients with pictures of 100 different products from 100 different companies without first educating those people in what is necessary.

I built my own ideas about nutritional network-marketing companies based on what I had seen in the past. I often thought to myself, if there were a way to simplify this approach, I would consider network-marketing. If we could just give limited choices based off of the immediate needs of someone trying to begin a weight loss journey, I am game. An athlete should already have some of this general knowledge.

What if someone has an option to purchase what they ACTUALLY need? Rather than confusing them with flashy labels of things they may lean towards "wanting" instead.

Were it not for my decision to join my first MLM opportunity, which set me on this path, this book would not be in your possession. My organization would not have experienced the growth it did. My ideas would not have turned the direction they did. I could very well still be a broke trainer, trying to change the world with an idea rather than real goals. Just about everything you have read up until this point was caused by and made capable of reaching, through my decision to go the network-marketing route. When I was introduced to my first opportunity, my mind was changed. And I was not going to allow fear or misinformation to hold me back any longer. You are really only able to change your mind once you are capable of using your mind.

Not to mention, it may not have been the right time, before. There were times I had tried MLM in the past. I always believed in the compensation programs behind network-marketing companies, but never the products, or even myself. I realized, for every before and after picture you see, many people are capitalizing from the results. Trainers, nutritionists, supplement companies… How much of that capital are you pocketing?

I was introduced much like anyone else. A friend sent me a message. Not just any message, rather, one of those – here is the universe giving me a chance to get out of this cycle, messages.

"Hey, can you meet me here at 3? Got this thing I want you to see." I knew what the "thing" was. I knew it was MLM. I knew there was going to be a buy-in. I knew I was broke. The funny thing was though, at that point in my life, I didn't care about those things.

I went to the shindig in a hotel conference room, right down the street from my home. Very convenient. I even took this as a sign. The man who introduced me to the opportunity was the very same man who was responsible for putting me in front of my first group of people to tell my story. So I definitely knew this was a sign.

He was there to meet me when I walked in, and since I hadn't seen him in months, we spent a few minutes catching up before the presentation began. I realized... An opportunity will not present itself unless you are supposed to act upon it or learn from it.

Then I saw, what I considered to be a trainer's dream opportunity. A chance at creating a real business with a little "out of the box" thinking. A way for every single client to become a huge asset for a trainer, building a lucrative business with multiple streams of passive income. A way to build real wealth instead of a (meager) generous salary.

So why this company? It eliminated the 3 biggest problems I saw as a trainer, and combined them into a nice logical package with a great message.

Clients need a goal – if you are not training for anything, you are exercising for nothing. Clients who are "starting out" don't need mountains of supplements – just a few basic necessities. Clients still want to eat crap before bed.

And the beauty… just by sticking to your goal, the company donated meal replacements to children fighting obesity.

Meal replacements with all of your essential vitamins, minerals, protein and fiber – that taste like dessert? And when your client reaches their weight loss goal, the company donates healthy meals to a child fighting obesity whose parents cannot afford healthy meals? Wow.

One of the tools I kept in my arsenal, as a trainer, was a goal contract. I would give a client 90 days in order to reach a goal. If that goal was met, the client was typically rewarded with a free month of training. This is where value comes into play. Do not be concerned with giving out free training. Embrace giving out free training! How do you feel your client will react when they reach their goal and you reward them with your service for free? Just for doing what they said they were going to do. Focus on keeping your client pool full and happy, and make sure that free month gets blasted all over social media.

If the client were to miss the goal, they would owe me for an extra month of training. It worked well. I would rarely have clients miss a goal. It happened occasionally. And there were 2 instances when I had clients disappear rather than pay me, but the contract created an even bigger bond between my clients and I. It created a bigger bond between the clients themselves too. As far as the 2 clients that disappeared, more power to them.

I mentioned earlier… in the time I was training, I lost less than a dozen clients. I do not mean people who moved or people who couldn't afford training anymore. I am sure you can imagine that if a client could not afford training for a month or two, I didn't mind training them training for free.

There are always going to be people you do not see eye to eye with. I used to rate my happiness by the hour and if I wasn't happy at a certain time of day, it was usually because of the client I was working with. If you are unable to see past differences or if chemistry isn't there, let them go. If you have done something to make them unhappy, fix the problem. If the problem cannot be solved, let them let go of you.

You are always going to deal with plateaus. These times make you stronger as a trainer and problem solver. But a plateau is usually because of lack of a goal. A goal with generous, positive consequences.

I have found, not only do people need a goal; they need reasons to never want to give up on their goal. I will repeat that. Not only do people need a goal, they need reasons, to never feel the desire to give up on their goal. If you know a child in need benefits from you reaching your goal? Suddenly, you have accountability on a completely different level.

It may have seemed illogical at the time, and it was a HUGE risk, so I put my plan into action. I approached all of my clients with my business idea and my vision. Rather than my clients paying me, I would have them pay a one-time fee to become a promoter for my company. Then teach them how to duplicate the system.

You may say to yourself: if the client buys into the company rather than paying me, I will be missing out on my $300 a month. (example figure from earlier) Try to think a little bit bigger and see the whole picture.

Operation duplication is the key to MLM. You are given the opportunity to turn a client into $500 a month... or $1500 a month. A year from now, those clients could very well be making you $50,000 per year. Or $1,000,000 per year, each! Think as big as you can, then take action even bigger!

Some of my clientele were apprehensive, and I was okay with that. I am still learning many lessons in MLM. One of them is, you absolutely cannot care about or think about what other people think of you. You have to start dreaming big again. Be willing to work your butt off for whatever you want, and willingly accept a loss in social status if necessary.

# CHAPTER 13

## OPPORTUNITY

## "KNOWLEDGE IS BLISS. IGNORANCE IS MISSED OPPORTUNITY."

You are already a network-marketer. You are already going out there and finding leads and attracting new customers to your business. You are already expanding a network of individuals to purchase your service. But, there is a trap you can fall into by being self-employed. And the trap can be worse than that of an employed person. Thinking too much about the future while never having enough capital to expand, comes to mind.

What happens if you need employees? How can you come up with a solid business plan so a bank will give you a loan? Why do you feel you need a loan? If you were to acquire a loan, what is the next step? What if you are turned down? How do you expand without help? The answer, regardless of which stance you want to take, comes back to under-capitalization. You do not have enough leads, enough customers, enough sales, enough feedback, or enough money to be where you want to be. Your business was created on an idea, but now reality has kicked in and you all too often think to yourself, it may be easier to go back to working for someone else again.

What if you could add assets without adding salaries? What about low-overhead solutions? You are waiting for your big break… what do you think that big break will be? How long do you think you will play out this existing pattern you are in before success just happens to you? Or do you think you may have to do something completely unbelievable? It would seem as though, if you want something you have never had before, you have to perform actions you have never thought to perform before.

The average job, which accounts for a majority of the populous, has a starting point where the result is already placed in front of the employee. They are then taught how to mimic the result. This behavior then produces thoughts in the subconscious mind, which produce feelings about the thought. These feelings drive the person into action. These actions cycle back to the original result. This behavior is continually repeated until the mind is forced to revert back to the original cycle, rather than finding innovative solutions to create a better result.

When people have the ability to choose or create for themself, they are forced to come up with an idea. The idea then produces thoughts, which create feelings of emotion about the idea. These feelings then drive them into action. These actions produce their very own result, based upon their original creative idea. Rather than being told to mimic the result from the beginning, this cycle reverts back to the creation of more ideas, be it innovation, or entirely new paths to explore.

You should, as an entrepreneur, be willing and able to explore as many paths to multiple streams of income as possible. You should be able to expand your business and your name at any moment, even if that means acting against the status quo. One big difference I see between a network-marketer and the average self-employed person, is the network-marketer is more than willing to speak to a perfect stranger about what they do, just for the sake of getting potential leads or sales. This is a mindset every entrepreneur must adopt in order to be successful in today's economy.

How easily can you prospect and gather leads to your business? Meaning, how simple is it to walk up to someone and attract him or her to your business or opportunity, without chasing him or her away or having someone immediately becoming skeptical? If you are in a room with a hundred random people, how many of those people can use your product or service? How many of those hundred can you close?

Network-marketing companies all relatively use the same approach. And the approach makes me sick. Hey kids – just go get 3 friends! And they get 3 friends! And they get 3 friends! And if you follow this model, you will become rich! Well, it sort of works that way. This is a simplistic way to approach it. You need to be taking the common sense route to joining a network-marketing company, and it will be your duty to show people this simple approach as well.

Your best approach is to market yourself and look at MLM as a solid business investment. And treat marketing yourself as a business too. If you are going to talk to someone once a month about your business, regardless of what business you are in, your rate of success will be directly proportionate to the amount of applied effort.

A large factor holding back success in MLM for most people is time. A person spending 4 to 8 hours a day, taking serious strides towards building their network, will get a lot further than someone talking about their business once a month. Is it by now, becoming more evident to you, that you already are in network-marketing to a degree, especially when it comes to being self-employed?

The market was saturated in the mid 1900's by a few very large companies. A new premise was born. Direct sales turned into a way of building residual income. There was a smaller population with less avenues to market and communicate themselves in.

There were less opportunities at the time to build wealth too. People actually loved and believed in the idea of network-marketing. They jumped at the idea of wearing buttons or knocking on doors. Why not? The vision was made clear and the compensation programs were sound and easily explainable.

So much so, that many companies popped up in the 80's and 90's, marketing this "easy as pie," get rich quick idea in many different fields. Marketing to varying demographics of people in many industries. The market became flooded. The people at the very top were making money. Those at the bottom were dropping like flies. Companies were going bankrupt as fast as they were being built. The entire idea of network-marketing was dying. It was becoming a bad taste in everyone's mouth. So much so, it placed a negative light on the idea for the following few generations of potential marketers.

Now, there are no jobs. There are kids getting out of college with a mountain of debt and nowhere to go. An entire generation of completely genius entrepreneurs and online marketers are beginning to realize they can earn more before the age of thirty, than their predecessors made in a lifetime. Thousands of times over. While you think it may be silly to collect even a single follower online, you have 18 year olds coming your way, with millions of followers and fans. How will you respond to the shift?

When these companies and kids collaborate and realize what is going on, they are going to leave a few older generations of business owners behind. What is happening is real. These companies are real. This shift in the economic climate is real. Multi-Level Marketing is here to stay, so get used to it.

By the time I realized this myself, I had already been invited to host seminars for a few other network-marketing companies. A presidential, superstar, awesome-sauce, coordinating director with one of these companies, (a gigantic one) had asked me to become a promoter for their company.

They offered to pay my buy-in and any startup expenses needed to get rolling hard. The industry calls this, enlisting a master distributor. It was a respectful position in a binary plan. (When someone goes south or drops out of a binary compensation plan, you create an opening for someone to move in. It only makes sense to offer these positions out to people of higher influence.) On top of being able to cash in on a few hundred thousand in volume on one leg, they offered to pay me a generous salary to travel, speak, and become a figurehead for a different outlook on their brand.

The salary didn't matter to me. The volume didn't matter to me. What mattered to me, I began seeing a bigger part of my destiny. I wasn't just a personal trainer anymore, putting on label-reading seminars at the local grocery store. I was an asset that people wanted. And I had the choice to help fulfill this destiny with any one of these companies. All the company was after all, was a tool to generate wealth. The wealth I desired to fuel my dreams of saving the world. Why not pick one that was right for me?

I felt this was my opportunity. The "opportunity," is the decision you are presented with, that can change your life... the instance to act upon. It isn't just a business presentation. It is the opening credits for a new chapter. Whenever you are presented with an opportunity to change your life, and fear onsets, you can do 1 of 2 things. You can succumb to it. Or you can overcome it. The anxiety you feel, the panic, the nausea, the shortness of breath. It is all a very great thing! What decision are you going to make? Which direction are you going to allow yourself to go from now on?

The point of this chapter was not to talk you into joining my team or my opportunity, although, we are always looking to create more leaders in our organization. The point is to shine some light on some new ideas, so you can align yourself with an opportunity. Now. Sign up, learn the business, and build your freedom!

Find a company that suits your personality. Find a leader who will hold your hand to victory. We are going to keep innovating our systems, and spreading our networks across the globe. And we are going to make a completely new generation of future leaders and role-models for the network-marketing industry to look up to, all while building passive income and making new friends and family in the process. I am pretty sure, by the time you read this, I will be a trillionaire, or well on my way! Oh yeah, and I must go run for mayor, too. I have a lot of work and campaigning to do!

# CHAPTER 14

# A QUICK OVERVIEW OF THE 3 LAWS

# "IF YOU EVER HAVE THE OPPORTUNITY TO WAKE UP, YOU WILL FIND IT DIFFICULT TO GO BACK TO SHEEP."

There are so many laws that govern our universe. On this leg of my journey, I stayed focused on the following 3. Read, and apply. Not just these laws, but everything else you have read in this book, too.

## The Law of Attraction

The Law of Attraction refers to like energies

attracting like energies. If someone wants something in their life, their need to match their vibrational frequency to resonate on like frequencies with what it is they want, in order to receive it, or, in order for there to be an attraction. In order for us to be attracted to one another we must also take into account there being zero coincidence in how and where we meet someone. We must instead realize, there is a purpose behind every decision we make and every step we take.

Imagine a man and a woman walking towards one another on an empty sidewalk. They are both having thoughts, both positive and negative, about a chance at an interaction between them. There could be doubt, fear, happiness, lust, etc., but they are having these thoughts because they are indeed sharing these thoughts. The closer they get to one another, the stronger the feelings become, and the more they feel pulled into, and connected to one another.

Now, imagine this is you... One or both of you can act upon the opportunity to say hello, and completely change your lives forever. Or you can pull your cell phone out of your pocket, or stare at the ground, and completely miss the chance at a life change.

The Law of Attraction has the word "action" imbedded in it. The Law of Attraction does not give us what we want. The Law of Attraction does not place us in front of people who will completely change our lives. The Law of Attraction brings us into alignment with these nouns, (persons, places, or things) and presents us with the opportunity to act upon them. To take action; and the result of the action is our life changing. It is, however, still our choice to take action.

**"Nothing happens until something moves." – Albert Einstein**

### The Law of Value

Give. To give is to receive. And getting what you pay for is simply receiving from what you give. Give without thinking. Give without expecting to receive anything. Most of our beliefs, when it comes to giving, come from our watching our parents give; or lack thereof. We are so quick to cast judgment at the homeless man on the street holding the sign. Or the person who approaches us at the gas station for a dollar. Regardless of what your ideas are of why that person may need your money, or what they will do with it, the universe is giving you the opportunity to let go of your past and live in the present moment without judgment. And in turn, possibly enact a positive butterfly effect in the ripple of time and space.

You must want to give. Although it might sound like a path to bankruptcy, to give more than you receive, you must have a different understanding of value. Value is not the same thing as price. Price is the cost of something. Value, is what determined your desire to purchase something. What you perceived you would receive and you what you wanted to receive must have more value than the money in your pocket. When you are placing value on yourself, you are not giving monetarily so to speak; you are adding more value to the lives of the people you are serving. This causes wealth to attract itself to you.

Success and happiness come from the desire of wanting to help. Wanting to give. With a sick work ethic and desperation to serve other people. No one can put a price on the value you can give. You know you love to serve. You know how happy it makes you when you give to someone. Let go of your beliefs when it comes to giving, and give because you love to serve.

## The Law of Compensation

Money is our reward for the value we have given to other people. A person who is working in a fast food restaurant is broke because they are working in a fast food restaurant. The billionaire who owns multiple companies, which give generous salaries to thousands of employees, is a billionaire, because he own multiple companies, which give generous salaries to thousands of employees. These may seem like paradoxes, and it is because that is exactly what they are.

The Law of Compensation states we are rewarded in direct proportion to the amount of value placed upon the service we have provided to other people… to the world or universe overall. Work, in the general sense of the word, is not service. Service is the gift or gifts you have within you that you can share with the world. Money is the reward for your service. Directly correlated to the amount of value placed in the service being performed. If you want to raise your compensation, raise the level of value, being placed on your level of contribution, to mankind. If you are broke, you are not adding enough value to enough people. If you want to become wealthy, provide more value to more people. If you want to become wealthy overnight – provide more value to more people overnight.

The universe is always in balance and will give you what you have worked your ass off for, and what you deserve. Not what you think you deserve. We attract what we feel. Not what we want.

When the Titanic struck that iceberg, a weary crewman ran to find people to help him construct lifeboats. He came across 3 types of passengers. The first ones said, "yes, we will help you build life boats!" The second said nothing… just stood there, almost like a deer in headlights. The third said, "The Titanic is unsinkable."

There are 3 types of people on this planet. Those who make things happen. Those who watch things happen. And those who say, "What just happened?"

Which of the three are you?

Go change the world. Go change yourself.

# ABOUT THE AUTHOR

Here is the content of the cover page for our first Wellness by Jason Newsletter. Be sure you find Wellness by Jason online and help us spread our message of change. Contact us to schedule a seminar or to become a part of our growing success and leadership teams.

**Community is different. Cities don't have borders. We don't have lines or labels. No country or religion. We only think of these things when we turn on the television (tell-a-vision). When people place ideas in our heads. Not when we are shopping in the store... or even watching our children play in the park. In these perfect moments - we have one another. Our neighbors and friends. Family and loved ones. Ask someone who has lived through a tragedy that affected a large group of people. We leave all material ideals**

aside, and bring forth compassion of the human soul.

We will all follow the speed limit - however, we have forgotten about the laws which govern the very universe we live in. One law specifically, is the law of compensation - which states - you will be rewarded in direct proportion to the amount of service you have done for others, in the past. Think for a second... if money is the reward you receive as payment for SERVICE you are doing for the rest of humanity, and you are broke - you haven't done enough service for others. Not work - work is self-service. And work is the worst way to receive compensation for service. That means you need to get out there, and do more, for other people.

Spend this year finding your passion. The completed 'wholeness' of you, is here to give in the greatest capacity you perceive as possible. What can you give, that will change your universe and the world around you? Give as God gives. Serve in the grandest way. If you want to increase your compensation, you need to increase the VALUE of your contribution to all of man.

We are far from perfect. We have all tried and failed. Been spoon fed the wrong information decade after decade. We want truth. And we should not have to go through piles of junk and lies to finally find the answers. We are specialists. Teachers. Blue and white collar workers. Public educators. Doctors. Nurses. Parents. Co-workers.

Friends. We are in the news. We make the news. We are average, everyday people. We are masters of our universe. We are you; with a common goal.

Wellness by Jason was created to re-educate society in falling out of cyclical behavior which holds us back from being the greatest versions of ourselves. Our initiative is to help bring together a closer, healthier community - give free education to all who want it - and give an opportunity, for all, to help others. Our purpose is to create, not followers - but a new generation of leaders. It is because of our failure, that we are now masters; masters whom succeed.

We are masters because we realize there is no ending. We are masters because, as we learn more and more, we realize just how little we know. Modern day education has taught us to achieve mastery of a chosen curriculum. We were never given the opportunity to learn about our "self". We must pursue mastery of our "self" to reach success.

Mastery is not a conclusion, but a practice that never stops. Success is a goal that is forever sought and never reached. Our "self" is an evolving and learning mind of our inner child, that can never be mastered. We can only become aware of our "self" and pursue education that will allow our thoughts, feelings, and emotions to align, and help us achieve this pursuit of the mastery of success. We must become aware of mastery having no ending - that education is a

**continuous practice of success.**

**Education has nothing to do with taking tests and becoming a master at memorization - it is about teaching people to become the dreamers they used to be, before their education began.**

Talking to an 8 year NFL veteran about the Project10 Challenge and Wellness by Jason.

"…with Wellness by Jason, you have the opportunity to have the mentorship, the team support, the camaraderie, and the family values we are trying to instill; and the culture that we want to instill on this team…"

One of Wellness by Jason's clients, commenting on a television broadcast about what Wellness by Jason has done for the City of Irving, Texas.

"…he has been a wonderful example for me. Jason was heavy at one time and that motivated me to work with him. He has just really helped me feel good about how long it has taken me to get healthy; and to just keep doing something every day… and I've definitely gotten to where I feel better; I have lost 25 pounds, and I'm on the road to being healthy."

Look us up online to see who said it! See you around!